Restorative Commons: Creating Health and Well-being through Urban Landscapes

Edited by

Lindsay Campbell and Anne Wiesen
U.S. Forest Service,   Meristem
Northern Research Station

General Technical Report NRS-P-39

Proceedings

The findings and conclusions of each article in this publication are those of the individual author(s) and do not necessarily represent the views of the U.S. Department of Agriculture or the Forest Service. All articles were received in digital format and were edited for uniform type and style. Each author is responsible for the accuracy and content of his or her paper.

Trademark

The use of trade, firm, or corporation names in this publication is for the information and convenience of the reader. Such use does not constitute an official endorsement or approval by the U.S. Department of Agriculture or the Forest Service of any product or service to the exclusion of others that may be suitable.

ISBN 978-0-16-086416-2

Published by
USDA Forest Service
Northern Research Station
11 Campus Blvd., Suite 200
Newtown Square, PA 19073

January 2009
Revised January 2011

Visit our homepage at:
http://www.nrs.fs.fed.us

For sale by
Superintendent of Documents,
U.S. Government Printing Office
Internet: bookstore.gpo.gov
Phone: toll free (866) 512-1800
         DC area (202) 512-1800
Fax: (202) 512-2104
Mail: Stop IDCC, Washington, DC 20402-0001

Designed by
Pure+Applied, New York

Contents

Case Studies

Interviews

Appendices

Reciprocity
Children from Martin
Luther King, Jr. Recreation
Center in Franklin Square
visit Gwynns Falls/Leakin
Park, Baltimore, MD (1995).
PHOTO USED WITH PERMISSION
BY PHOTOGRAPHER STEFFI GRAHAM

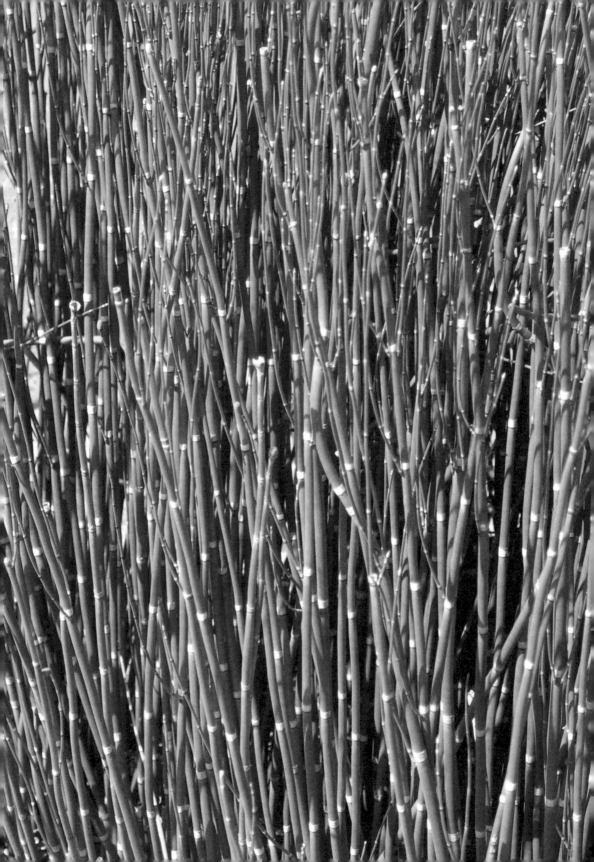

Foreword

All of us have had the experience of walking through a
garden, by a river or ocean, or climbing a mountain and
finding ourselves simultaneously calmed and reinvigorated,
engaged in mind, refreshed in body and spirit. The
importance of these physiological states on individual
and community health is fundamental and wide-ranging.
In 40 years of medical practice, I have found two types of
non-pharmaceutical "therapy" vitally important for patients
with chronic neurological diseases: music and gardens.
I have recently been thinking and writing a lot about music
and I have just published a book called "Musicophilia" —
a title I chose as a reference to E. O. Wilson's term "biophilia."
Indeed, I think there is a biological need and craving that
goes across all cultures and all times both for music and
for greenness. I would even suggest that a sort of subtype
of biophilia may be *hortophilia*, or a special desire for
gardens. I can't quite claim that hortophilia is in the genes
because, of course, gardens have only existed presumably
since the beginnings of agriculture. But I have often seen
the restorative and healing powers of nature and gardens,
even for those who are deeply disabled neurologically.
In many cases, gardens and nature are more powerful
than any medication.

I have one friend with moderately severe Tourette's syndrome —
in his usual, busy, city environment, he has thousands of tics and
verbal ejaculations each day — grunting, jumping, touching things
compulsively. I was therefore amazed once when we were hiking
in a desert to realize that his tics had completely disappeared. The
remoteness and uncrowdedness of the scene, combined with some
ineffable calming effect of nature, served to defuse his ticcing, to
"normalize" his neurological state, at least for a time.

Another patient, an elderly lady with Parkinson's disease, often
found herself "frozen," unable to initiate movement — a common
problem for those with parkinsonism. But once we led her out into the
garden, where plants and a rock garden provided a varied landscape,
she was galvanized by this and could rapidly, unaided, climb up the
rocks and down again.

I have often seen patients with very advanced dementia or
Alzheimer's disease, who may have very little sense of orientation to
their surroundings. They have often forgotten, or cannot access, how to
tie their shoes or handle cooking implements. But put them in front of a
flowerbed with some seedlings, and they will know exactly what to do —
I have never seen such a patient plant something upside down.

The patients I see often live in nursing homes or chronic-care
institutions for decades, and so the physical environment of these
settings is crucial in promoting their well-being. A number of these
institutions have actively used the design and management of their
open spaces to promote better health for their patients. For example,
Beth Abraham Hospital in the Bronx, New York (which opened in 1920
for the first victims of the sleeping sickness — encephalitis lethargica)
is where I saw the severely parkinsonian post-encephalitic patients of
"Awakenings." At that time the hospital was a pavilion surrounded by
large gardens. As it expanded to a 500-bed institution, it swallowed
most of its gardens, but it did retain a central patio full of potted plants
that remains very crucial for the patients. There are also raised beds
so that blind patients can touch and smell and wheelchair patients can
have direct contact with the plants. I also work with the Little Sisters of
the Poor, who have nursing homes all across the world. This is an order
originally founded in Brittany in the late 1830s, and it spread to America
in the 1860s. At that time it was common for an institution like a nursing

home to have a large garden and sometimes a dairy as well. Alas, this is
a tradition which has mostly vanished, but which the Little Sisters are
trying to reintroduce today. At the Little Sisters of the Poor in Queens,
when it becomes warm enough, all of the residents like to be out in the
garden. Some of them can walk by themselves, some need a stick, some
need a walker, and some have to be wheeled. But they all want to be in
the garden.

Clearly, nature calls to something very deep in us, and biophilia,
the love of nature and living things, is an essential part of the human
condition. Hortophilia, the desire to interact with, manage, and tend
nature, is also deeply instilled in us. The role that nature plays in
health and healing becomes even more critical for people working
long days in windowless offices, for those living in city neighborhoods
without access to green spaces, for children in city schools, or those
in institutional settings such as nursing homes. The effects of nature's
qualities on health are not only spiritual and emotional, but physical
and neurological. I have no doubt that they reflect deep changes in the
brain's physiology, and perhaps even its structure. As a physician, I take
my patients to gardens whenever possible; as a writer, I find gardens
essential to the creative process.

I was honored to give the keynote address at the first Meristem
Restorative Commons Forum in 2007 and I am honored to introduce this
volume, which is inspired by that conference. The proceedings from the
Forum, and related case studies included here, mark an important step
in fostering new interdisciplinary collaborations in the design and use of
common urban green spaces to support public health and well-being.

Oliver Sacks, M.D.
New York, NY

Preface

→ SEE APPENDICES PAGE 268

The **Meristem 2007 Forum**, "Restorative Commons for Community Health", introduced the concept of *Restorative Commons* as a broad vision for 21st century urban open space. Convened at the New York Academy of Medicine, the Forum organized thought leaders and practitioners from the fields of health (medicine, psychology, social epidemiology), design (urban planning, landscape architecture, and architecture), and urban natural resource management to give specificity and meaning to this vision. Through presentations of research, theoretical frameworks, design processes, built examples, programmatic innovations, and clinical experience, some basic considerations for creating public spaces conducive to individual and community health began to emerge. Participants asserted that these spaces should be accessible, especially to vulnerable populations; should respond to needs at the neighborhood level; and should create opportunities for social engagement, economic empowerment, nature access, and stewardship. They are community-driven, ecologically sustainable, and answer the very human impulse to seek and create beauty in our everyday surroundings. They are a primary foundation for a resilient community. Facilitated sessions revealed a need to expand this dialogue and inspired the creation of this volume.

This volume is a joint endeavor of Meristem and the U.S. Forest Service Northern Research Station to explore the relationship between human health and the urban environment. Both organizations are working to strengthen networks of researchers and practitioners to develop new solutions to persistent and emergent challenges to human health, well-being, and potential within the urban environment.

Culled from the Meristem Forum presentations, participant contributions and additional innovators in the above-named fields, this volume documents compelling practices and principles that are currently utilized to create Restorative Commons — either as small-scale experiments or as larger efforts to "institutionalize innovation". It includes academic writing of researchers in the fields of medical history, evolutionary biology, and urban planning. And it couples this writing with practitioners' experiential knowledge presented as essays, thought pieces, and interviews. Thought pieces written by architects are short essays intended to provoke reflection on changes in urban infrastructure. Case studies present reflections and lessons learned from both the practitioner and the research perspectives. Interviews provide a vehicle for practitioners who are busy in the day-to-day operations of their field programs to share their insights and points of view from their on-the-ground experiences. The photographs and design drawings are intended not just as illustrations to the text, but as data that communicate what cannot be conveyed through words.

In the way that Oliver Sacks uses the clinical case study as a rich means of communicating insight, we believe that there is value for research and practitioner communities in sharing case-based innovations. When describing interactions between complex systems (such as the urban built environment, socio-cultural systems, globalized economic systems, the biosphere) particularly at the neighborhood or city scale, it is necessary to draw on equally nuanced evidence. Experimental, quasi-experimental, and quantitative data alone are necessary but not sufficient to understand the interactions of the urban ecosystem. There is also a need for textured, qualitative narratives that convey the *how* behind the relationships that catalyze and the mechanisms that produce change. To that end, narratives in this volume include first-hand accounts of project participants and impassioned voices of community leaders speaking of their own work in their own

Previous Page:
New York City Housing Authority community garden, Boston Secor Houses, Bronx, NY.
PHOTO USED WITH PERMISSION BY PHOTOGRAPHER LLOYD CARTER, NYCHA

neighborhoods; systemic reflections of program directors; and research that explores the significance of the Restorative Commons.

Throughout the volume contributors offer an informal dialogue about the development of their vision, discussing what inspires them personally in a parallel text noted in the margin. We asked several practitioners to respond to the writing of a colleague whose work reinforces or contrasts their own, in an effort to promote dialogue and mutual learning. Because programs are comprised not just of good ideas and principles, but also of tangible resources (human, financial, material) and organizational strategies, attempts are made throughout this compendium to describe the evolution of projects and their critical resources, partnerships, and turning points along the way.

Because the Meristem Forum was designed to convene New York City leadership, the cases in this volume are also largely rooted in the city's landscape. We asked speakers to write about the work they presented as informed by their subsequent reflections upon the Forum. Despite the strong New York City focus, the recurrence of ecological site types and the common concerns that these programs are designed to address broadened our research (to Connecticut, Massachusetts, New Jersey, Ohio, and one international example) and ensures this work's relevance to a broader public. The observations of practitioners and writings of theorists echo each other's recognition of the primacy of *citizen stewardship* and creative *design* in developing new health-promoting environments. Brief summaries of findings and new questions raised in the context of these themes are offered in the introduction.

Acknowledgments

We thank Dr. Oliver Sacks for sharing his passion for gardens, his compassion for human vulnerability, and his ability to catalyze collaboration between New York City agencies, organizations, and individuals at the Meristem 2007 Forum.

We offer special recognition and gratitude to David Kamp, FASLA, LF, a founder of Meristem, and co-organizer and co-convener of the Meristem 2007 Forum.

For their sustained enthusiasm, intellectual underwriting, and outreach to their network of experts in urban health, design, and natural resources management, we thank Robert Martensen, John Seitz, Jeffery Sugarman, and Erika Svendsen.

We thank our project funders: The Harvard-Loeb Fellowship Forum, David Kamp FASLA, LF of Dirtworks, PC Landscape Architecture, Institute for Landscape Studies, Terrapin Bright Green, and a generous individual who wishes to remain anonymous. Without all these partners the Forum would have been impossible.

We dedicate this work to the health, well-being, vitality, and resilience of New York City — our home.

The commons represent both the natural systems (water, air, soil, forests, oceans, etc.) and the cultural patterns and traditions (intergenerational knowledge ranging from growing and preparing food, medicinal practices, arts, crafts, ceremonies, etc.) that are shared without cost by all members of the community.

—Ecojustice Dictionary
2008

The very notion of the commons implies a resource is owned, managed, and used by the community. A commons embodies social relations based on interdependence and cooperation. There are clear rules and principles; there are systems of decision-making. Decisions...are made jointly and democratically by members of the community.

—Vandana Shiva
2005

Introduction

Lindsay Campbell
U.S. Forest Service, Northern Research Station

Anne Wiesen
Meristem

The collection of writings presented in this volume offer a starting point for a multidisciplinary understanding of *Restorative Commons*. Although the notion of commons is broad and includes natural commons, such as the atmosphere, international waters, and rangeland; as well as information commons from folktales and myths to freeware and shareware; we focus here on open space and its interface with the built environment. For open space to function as a *commons*, it should be publicly accessible, nonexcludable, and managed through shared governance. We consider sites *restorative* if they contribute to the health and well-being of individuals, communities, and the landscape. Individual health includes physical, mental, emotional, and social health; community health is considered in terms of rights, empowerment, and neighborhood efficacy; and landscape health is measured by ecosystem function and resilience — all of which act together in a complex web of relationships.

Vandana Shiva (2005) argues that democracy and environmentalism have mutual underpinnings in ubiquitous models of common natural resource management across time and cultures. There are long legacies as well as substantial contemporary efforts in community stewardship in both rural, developing contexts (such as community forestry in Nepal and Bhutan; peasant farming in India; or cooperative ecotourism in Namibia) and urban contexts (such as the Urban Resources Initiative programs in Baltimore and New Haven discussed here). It is no coincidence that these interventions are successful at a local scale. The notion of a global commons seems almost untenable, and potentially susceptible to the "tragedy of the commons" or the failures of collective action among large groups (Hardin 1968, Olson 1971). However, at the localized scale, social institutions, myths, mores, norms of reciprocity, kinship, and community ties can enable the development of sustainably managed commons. There is evidence in a variety of contexts of enduring common property regimes that successfully manage natural resources through shared, local decision-making (see, for example, Ostrom 1990). Thus, this volume emphasizes cases and models of community-based, civic stewardship.

Parks, community gardens, building exteriors, rights-of-way, botanical gardens, urban farms, vacant lots, public housing campuses, and closed landfills offer unique opportunities for restoring social and ecological function in the public, urban sphere. These fragments of the commons must be considered as individual and unique, and simultaneously as parts of a larger system. Even a jail's yard can serve as a restorative space for the inmates and staff. Cooperation with land owners, developers, designers, building managers, and tenants will be required to work creatively at the critical junctures where public meets private urban land: including apartment and office building interiors, front yards, and rooftops. Humans are unique in that we actively participate in creating conditions for our own health through the design of our buildings, neighborhoods, and cities at a global scale. Thus, innovative design is a key approach for building Restorative Commons.

Human Health and Well-being

The notion of linking human health and the form and function of open space is not new. For example, Robert Martensen discusses how American landscape architects of the 19th century developed parks in collaboration with medical expertise to positively influence public health even when relationships between environments and disease were not fully understood and mechanisms were under-theorized. While the development of germ theory unlocked many mysteries about the spread and treatment of disease, it is worth considering what may also have been lost by abandoning our more holistic understanding of "salubrity" and beneficial environments. Without full understanding of the causal mechanisms between mental and physical health and local environments, can we design spaces guided by the precautionary principle? Can we use our intuition — and perhaps even our evolutionary impulses—as guides toward what sorts of environments are vital to promoting health and quality of life, such as access to sunlight, water, clean air, and vegetative diversity? Evolutionary psychologist Judith Heerwagen details elemental features of nature that convey feelings of safety, opportunity, connection, and pleasure in our environment. Both the foreword of Dr. Oliver Sacks and the broader work of biophilic design theory suggest that positive references to our shared evolutionary heritage in the design of our current habitats can confer psychological benefits and promote healing at the neurological level in ways we are just beginning to understand (Kellert et al. 2008).

As the absence of disease in human life does not constitute health (WHO 1946) so, too, the absence of contamination in our environment does not constitute environmental health. Indeed, the World Health Organization's constitution defines human health as "the state of complete physical, mental, and social well-being and not merely the absence of disease or infirmity." Can we craft an equally complete definition for environmental health? Global climate change impacts and the accompanying encroachment of new and resurgent diseases illuminate our vulnerability and the intimacy of the health of our land, the health of our communities, and strength of our relationships within our community. Wendell Berry (1994) writes:

> "If we speak of a healthy community, we cannot be speaking
> of a community that is merely human. We are talking about a
> neighborhood of humans in a place, plus the place itself: its soil,
> its water, its air, and all the families and tribes of the nonhuman
> creatures that belong to it. What is more, it is only if this whole
> community is healthy ...[and] the human economy is in practical
> harmony with the nature of the place, that its members can
> remain healthy and be healthy in body and mind and live in a
> sustainable manner."

How do we proceed to expand our definition of health to include the health of the land and further, to invest in the health of our landscapes as part of our healthcare programs? What would it look like for a hospital to steward the land it inhabits and that of the neighborhood it serves?

Current research in health-related fields reveals patterns in human healing processes that affirm the experiences recounted in the cases

Without full understanding of the causal mechanisms between mental and physical health and local environments, can we design spaces guided by the precautionary principle?

studies of this volume. Psychoneuroimmunology, the study of connections between psychological states and the nervous, endocrine, and immune systems, tells us that "mind-body interactions are so ubiquitous that it may no longer be possible to refer to body and mind as separate entities" (Lerner 1994). This means that our physical health, safety and welfare may profoundly affect our emotional and mental health, including our ability to form relationships, to conduct productive work, and to enjoy recreation. Reciprocally, emotional states of mind and behavioral patterns may profoundly affect our physiological health. (Lerner 1994). Further, studies of trauma survivors suggest that people become traumatized not by a catastrophic event alone, but by the ensuing breach in a former relationship or community of *safety, connection, acceptance*, and *empowerment* (Herman 1997). Can we design public places that elicit feelings of security and connection? If we invite activities that foster experiences of acceptance and empowerment, can we build places that strengthen community health?

We also consider the notion that health outcomes are tied to the *impacts of our social and economic status*. One public health theory holds that "social conditions and self-management are more powerful determinants of health than access to care" (Pincus 1998). An editorial in the American Journal of Public Health states:

> "That certain conditions commonly referred to as social determin-
> ants — including access to affordable healthy food, potable water,
> safe housing, and supportive social networks — are linked to health
> outcomes is something on which most of us can agree. The unequal
> distribution of these conditions across various populations is
> increasingly understood as a significant contributor to persistent and
> pervasive health disparities. If attention is not paid to these conditions,
> we will most surely fail in our efforts to eliminate health disparities."
> (Baker et al. 2005)

Many of the cases in this volume describe programs that are built on the above assumption. How can we continue to build from these models to create local economic systems that are rooted in stewardship of the urban environment? Can socioeconomic status be improved *in situ*, at the neighborhood scale, without causing gentrification and displacement? What are the limits to what natural resource management can accomplish?

Finally, there are both ends-based and rights-based reasons for considering the health of the natural environment. As health is increasingly recognized as a human right, environmental health that promotes human health and well-being is also being considered by some as a human right (Earthjustice 2004, Taylor 2004).

Civic Stewardship

As the human population in both the United States and globally becomes — for the first time — more urban than rural, new approaches to urban planning, urban design, social service delivery, and the management of open spaces, are required. To that end, local governments have demonstrated ability to lead, as exemplified by the 127 initiatives in New York City Mayor Michael Bloomberg's long-term sustainability plan known as PlaNYC 2030. This plan has fostered a new era in development of parks and open space in New York City, and dedicated the most resources to parks creation and maintenance since the time of Robert Moses. Unlike that period, a new understanding of citizen knowledge and shared governance has shaped the values and methods of urban planning. From the individual citizen pruner, to the block association beautification committee, to the community garden, to the parks conservancy group, and to the nonprofit land trust — civil society has articulated a wide array of responses at many scales addressing the management of the urban ecosystem. Many innovations in the design and maintenance of parks and the public rights-of-way were inspired by the pioneering work of civic groups that sought creative solutions to old neighborhood-based problems.

This publication focuses largely on programs that encourage citizen stewardship and caretaking of the land as a means to promoting health. Perhaps the "hortophilia" that Oliver Sacks posits does indeed exist. Or perhaps, as Erika Svendsen suggests, there is something basic and important for the quality of human life in the ability to create change in the physical environment. The significance of citizen self-help through environmental stewardship is explored through the practitioner writings of Edie Stone, Colleen Murphy-Dunning, and Rob Bennaton. As sustainability interventions move from plan, to policy, to implementation, they will rest on the engaged actions of citizen stewards. One million newly planted trees will not survive without constituents to care for them; community supported agriculture cannot exist without its members; farmers' markets require consumers; and green buildings require tenants. In essence, the urban ecosystem cannot function without citizen engagement.

Stewardship consists not only of physical land management, but also of longer-term engagement in education and advocacy. Experiential, field-based environmental education is taking myriad forms that occur off school grounds, sometimes with formal classroom partners and sometimes without. A recent assessment of New York City stewardship groups conducted by the Forest Service Northern Research Station (STEW-MAP) found that 83 percent of these groups say that they aim to educate friends, neighbors, and representatives about the environment and 38 percent say that their *primary* focus is "education"—which was second only to "environment" (Svendsen et al. 2008). A number of the projects profiled in this publication focus on education, employment, and capacity building. Ian Marvy offers a model of youth empowerment, local economy, and food justice at Added Value's Red Hook Community Farm; James Jiler teaches horticulture and job-readiness through the Rikers Island Prison Horticulture Program; Susan Lacerte discusses culturally specific educational events that were developed with and for the most diverse county in America at the Queens Botanic Garden. Human health and well-being are intimately connected to a sense of agency that can be cultivated through education and community organizing, particularly when focusing on underserved populations, such as youths, racial and ethnic minorities, inmates, or ex-offenders.

Open space stewardship is being used in response to grave tragedies such as war, ethnic conflict, and loss of human life—pushing the boundaries of how we believe natural resources can be used. Surely, gardens cannot solve the problem of war, but they do offer tools for reconciliation, rebuilding, and self-reliance, even in the most devastated of environments, as shown by Davorin Brdanovic's Bosnia and Herzegovina community garden program. These gardens provide not only income and food security, but they also serve as common, unprogrammed space—as a space in which people once divided by war can come together on their own terms. The Living Memorials

Project research shows the way in which hundreds of individuals, community groups, and towns chose to use trees and open space in remembrance of September 11, 2001, as a way of marking a tragic event and reflecting on the cycle of life. Lindsay Campbell's case study of the Brian Joseph Murphy Memorial Preservation Land probes how landscape can function as a living memorial, serving another basic human need — to remember.

These case studies offer new approaches to the old paradigm of "natural resource management." Are we witnessing the beginning of a new environmental stewardship ethic, one that moves us beyond 'control over', or even 'responsibility for', to an ethic based on mutual nourishment between people and the landscape? What are the inherent returns to our health and well-being that we receive by engaging in this reciprocal act of caring?

Design

Without attempting to define or categorize all types of ecological design, we highlight forms that create unique opportunities for social and ecological interactions at multiple scales, including the individual/experiential and the collective/systems level. We explore the development of biophilic and systems design and the codification of high performance infrastructure guidelines. We believe that the examples of public design documented in this volume achieve the efficiency of the green building movement, while retaining the "sensuous experience of nature" — to quote Hillary Brown. Brown contends that designers should create high performance buildings and infrastructure that take cues from natural features and systems. Further, Heerwagen encourages designers and decision-makers to "create places imbued with positive emotional experiences — enjoyment, pleasure, interest, fascination, and wonder —that are the precursors of human attachment to and caring for place."

Architects and landscape architects are generating rich, new models of buildings and open space that expose and explore human-environment relationships. For example, the Monroe Center for the Arts in Hoboken, NJ, emerges from Victoria Marshall's practice of "thinking about the nature we want to create." With her emphasis on processes, Marshall's design works to restore the function of whole systems.

Are we witnessing the beginning of a new environmental stewardship ethic based on mutual nourishment between people and the landscape?

Social Network
Map of the 2800 civic
stewardship groups in
New York City.

DATA SOURCE: STEW-MAP,
U.S. FOREST SERVICE UNPUBLISHED
DATA AS OF MAY 2008; MAP CREATED
BY JARLATH O'NEIL-DUNNE,
UNIVERSITY OF VERMONT

In this case, a building complex is designed to engage the Hudson River Estuary and the water cycle more generally in the daily lives and thus daily consciousness of the buildings' occupants. Marshall writes about the potential to cultivate stewards, so, too, does Susan Lacerte present the Queens Botanical Garden's (QBG) LEED platinum certified building, its publicly accessible green roof and on-site stormwater management system, and the broader QBG grounds as a site for ecological education. John Seitz recalls early efforts of earth artists and community gardeners to focus attention on nature and natural systems in New York City — introducing interactivity with the landscape, as opposed to prior models based more on creating pastoral viewsheds. These efforts helped to catalyze the current greening of infrastructure, by capturing public attention and imagination as to what might be possible.

David Kamp's designs show an attention to the variety of intimate impressions that all people can experience in a single space. Design considerations for the restorative garden at the Cleveland Botanical Garden were developed by Kamp and reflect collaboration with healthcare and horticultural therapy professionals. Indeed, we can think of David Kamp's garden designs as clinically informed approaches to many of the infirmities and disabilities that Sacks highlights in the foreword. While designed to accommodate the needs of those physically and mentally disabled, the garden ultimately is intended to engage all garden dwellers in healing benefits. In the words of Nancy Gerlach-Spriggs (1998), "…a Restorative Garden is intended by its planners to evoke rhythms that energize the body, inform the spirit and ultimately enhance the recuperative powers inherent in [the] body or mind."

This raises the important question, particularly in an urban context: How can we design with the broadest understanding of local needs? Jeff Sugarman offers the example of the redevelopment of Fresh Kills landfill into Fresh Kills Park. The project is a model in pioneering restorative/ecological design at a grand scale that responded first and foremost to community priorities and needs. The notion of participatory planning explored in Sugarman's case study brings design full circle to the notion of civic stewardship. Erika Svendsen illustrates that we can use open space not only to accommodate multiple users, or even respond to community priorities, but further, to strengthen social capital and foster resilience in our social systems.

This volume offers exemplary cases of designs that recognize the need to cultivate stewards and stewards working toward ecological design — design that is flexible, adaptive to use, and that exposes the relationships between people and their environments.

Lessons Learned and Persistent Questions

Collected together and considered as a body of data, certain principles begin to emerge across the research, programs, and sites explored here. To support healthy cities, we must engage with multiple open space site-types using systems thinking, while championing civic creativity and self-expression. Understanding the profound impacts of social and economic inequality on health outcomes, we must commit to social justice; promote social cohesion; tailor programs to serve diversely resourced communities; and cultivate local economic systems. Retaining the best of previous calls for sustainability, there is a need to support future generations through education and youth empowerment.

This publication also discusses challenges that prevent projects from realizing their fullest potential. It may indeed be the case that some of these innovations work best at the small scale and in a specific context. But if so, what does this mean for the broader urban environment and the population as a whole? And what components of models can be adapted from one site-type to another (green building to green infrastructure), from one discipline to another (ecology to public health), and from one nation to another (Bosnia to America)? An area for further exploration is the question of how programs can strike a productive balance between "expert" ecological and therapeutic design and the local knowledge of community based stewards. A final challenge arises from the issue of adaptability. Even the most thoughtfully designed space originates at a particular place and time. How should sites be designed to adapt to changing conditions and populations?

This volume is intended to provoke further debate. How can our basic human needs be respected in the development of our cities, including in the many new forms of emergent green infrastructure? Can we imagine the city as a mosaic of gardens — products of both nature and culture that serve both? What policies will help us to build the resilient communities we need to meet imminent challenges? What kind of nature do we want to create?

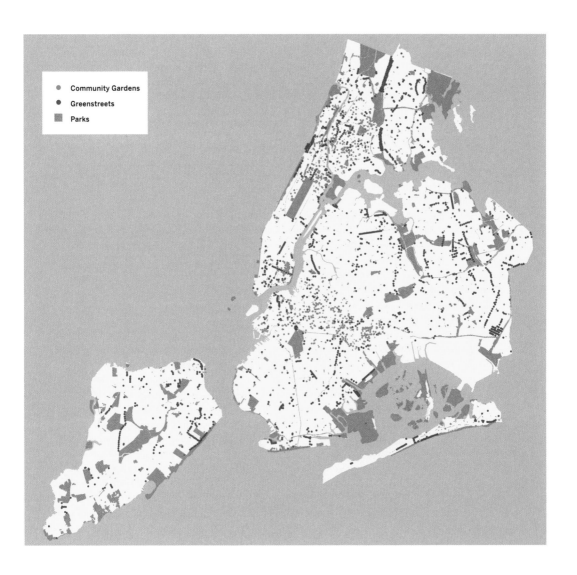

Legend:
- Community Gardens
- Greenstreets
- Parks

Green Infrastructure
Map of parks, community
gardens, and greenstreets
in New York City.
DATA SOURCE: NYC DEPT OF PARKS
AND RECREATION AND COUNCIL ON THE
ENVIRONMENT OF NEW YORK CITY; MAP
CREATED BY JARLATH O'NEIL-DUNNE,
UNIVERSITY OF VERMONT

Literature Cited

Baker, Elizabeth; Metzler, Marilyn; Galea, Sandro. 2005. Addressing social determinants of health inequities: learning from doing. American Journal of Public Health. 95(4): 553-558.

Berry, Wendell. 1993. Sex, economy, freedom & community: Eight essays. New York: Pantheon Books.

Center for Ecojustice Education. 2008. Ecojustice dictionary. Online resource: http://www.centerforecojusticeeducation.org/index. php?option=com_rd_glossary&Itemid=35. Accessed 1 July 2008.

Earthjustice. 2003. Human rights and the environment. Issue Paper for 60th Session of the United Nations Commission on Human Rights. Geneva. 15 March 2003-20 April 2004. 80 p.

Gerlach-Spriggs, N; Kaufman, R.E.; Warner, S.B. 1998. Restorative gardens: The healing landscape. New Haven: Yale University Press.

Hardin, Garrett. 1968. The tragedy of the commons. Science.162: 1243-1248.

Herman, Judith. 1997. Trauma and recovery: The aftermath of violence—from domestic abuse to political terror. New York: Basic Books.

Kellert, S.R.;Heerwagen, J.H.; Mador, M. 2008. Biophilic design: Theory, science, and practice. New York: Wiley.

Lerner, Michael. 1994. Choices in healing: integrating the best of conventional and complementary approaches to cancer. Cambridge, MA: MIT Press.

Olson, Mancur. 1971. The logic of collective action: Public goods and the theory of groups. Revised edition. Cambridge: Harvard University Press.

Ostrom, Elinor. 1990. Governing the commons. The evolution of institutions for collective action. Cambridge: Cambridge University Press.

Pincus, Theodore; Esther, Robert; DeWalt, Darren A. 1998. Social conditions and self-management are more powerful determinants of health than access to care. Annals of Internal Medicine. 129(5): 406-416.

Shiva, Vandana. 2005. Earth democracy: justice, sustainability and peace. Cambridge, MA: South End Press. 205 p.

Svendsen, Erika; Campbell, Lindsay; Fisher, Dana. 2008. Understanding urban environmental stewardship in New York City. In: Proceedings of the international symposium on society and resource management (ISSRM): Past and future; 2008 June 10-14; Burlington, VT. Burlington, VT: University of Vermont. Abstract.

Taylor, David. 2004. Is environmental health a basic human right?
Environmental Health Perspectives. 112(17): A1007-A1009

World Health Organization. 1946. World Health Organization constitution.
Online resource: http://www.who.int/governance/eb/who_constitution_
en.pdf. Accessed 21 July 2008.

Theory

Authors from three academic disciplines offer theoretical grounding for the Restorative Commons concept. From a historical perspective, we look to our immediate past for evidence of holistic practice in large scale urban park design and development. From evolutionary psychology, we are urged to recognize our needs and preferences for beneficial environments that are common and shared across humanity. And from urban planning, our attention is called to the health opportunities presented through citizen stewardship and management of urban open space. Understanding, creating, and sustaining the impacts of new 'green' forms in the urban sphere will continue to require cross- and interdisciplinary research.

Landscape Designers, Doctors, and the Making of Healthy Urban Spaces in 19th Century America

Robert Martensen, M.D., Ph.D.
National Institute of Health, Office of NIH History & Museum

During the middle decades of the 19th century, a loose collaborative of landscape designers and physicians looked to each other for ideas and support as they crafted an urban vision that combined environmental health, aesthetics, and a democratic *ethos* in a uniquely American mixture. From approximately 1840 to 1880, they crafted a health/environmental dualism that informed the design not only of large urban parks, which were then a contested public undertaking, but also of military encampments and hospitals, the one-room schoolhouse, 'rural' cemeteries, and early suburbs (Szcygiel and Hewitt 2000). My Meristem Forum presentation of March 30, 2007 discusses two of the movement's leaders — John Rauch, a Chicago physician whose environmental analyses shaped landforms of the Chicago park system, and his correspondent and muse, Frederick Law Olmsted, the leading landscape designer of the 19th century.

Olmsted, Rauch, and their collaborators made use of the predominant communicable disease conception of the pre-bacterio-logical-era — miasma theory — to guide their urban reforms. At its simplest, miasma theory, which has a history stretching back to the ancient Hippocratics and Vitruvius, assumes that the products of stagnation and decay, be they bad air, dirty water, or rotting meat and vegetables, account for most human afflictions. If stagnation and decay can be prevented at both physical and social levels, the argument ran, health is likely to ensue. For them, 'health' meant 'salubrity,' which is an

Previous Page:
New York City Housing Authority community garden, Marlboro Houses, Brooklyn, NY.
PHOTO USED WITH PERMISSION BY PHOTOGRAPHER LLOYD CARTER, NYCHA

Left:
Bethesda Fountain in Central Park was created to celebrate the completion of the Croton Aqueduct (1842), which for the first time provided all New Yorkers with clean drinking water. Crowning the fountain, The Angel of the Waters sculpture references the biblical angel who rendered the Pond of Bethesda healing water such that "whosoever stepped in were made whole of whatever disease he had." (John 5:4).
PHOTO USED WITH PERMISSION BY NEW YORK CITY PARKS PHOTO ARCHIVE. PHOTO BY ALAJOS L. SCHUSLER (1934)

ancient Latin word that suffuses discussions of environmental health
from Vitruvius in second century Rome onward through Ulysses S.
Grant's analysis of sites for potential military encampments.

According to Webster's Dictionary, "salubrity" means "favorableness
to the preservation of health" and "a quality of wholesomeness,
healthfulness." Any major environmental e lement — land form, water
moving and still, climate patterns, vegetation, wind patterns, history
of local epidemics — had its role to play in whether or not an observer
assessed a site as salubrious or not. Observers could judge an area
to be rich in agricultural potential, such as the Mississippi delta,
but insalubrious due to its poor drainage and history of pestilence,
for example. Historian Conovery Bolton Valencius (2002) recently
published a superb book, "The Health of the Country", that explores
how American settlers in the early 19th century often spoke in terms
of salubrity as they assessed the agricultural potential and sustainability
of various locations.

Nineteenth century city dwellers also employed a rhetoric of
salubrity. Unlike today, when the infant mortality rate in New York
City — 6.7 per 1,000 live births in 2007 — is lower than in many rural
and suburban areas, many large cities in the U.S. and Europe during
the early 19th century were so unhealthy that their populations could
not maintain themselves without substantial net in-migration from the
country. Even as wages for urban industrial workers began to rise in
the early 19th century, contemporary commentators noted that urban
environments were becoming less healthy than their 18th century
counterparts. New York City was less healthy than London, but even
along the Thames mortality rates for all decades worsened from 1815
to 1845. Writing on conditions in Manhattan in 1865, reformer Stephen
Smith lamented: "Here infantile life unfolds its bud, but perishes before
its first anniversary. Here youth is ugly with loathsome diseases and the
deformities which follow physical degeneracy. . . . The poor themselves
have a very expressive term for the slow process of decay which they
suffer, viz.: 'Tenement-house Rot'" (Szreter and Mooney 1998)

Chicago and Rauch

Chicagoans might be accumulating personal wealth, but an 1835
editorial in the "Chicago Democrat" bemoaned that, "The atmosphere

has already become poisoned" due to standing water that was "green" and "putrid" from decaying vegetable matter (Grob 2005). The cause was Chicago's natural situation, which consisted of a flat topography, high water table, and clay soils — all perceived by contemporaries as pre-disposing cause for miasmatic afflictions such as cholera. Chicago's early streets, for example, did not drain; instead, filth and water accumulated. To ameliorate the unhealthful effects of limited natural drainage, Chicago leaders in 1852 established a new street grade that necessitated raising Chicago's streets, an activity they repeated in 1857 and 1868 to counter perceptions that their roadways remained "too damp" and "unhealthful" (Pierce 1937-57).

Rauch, an early leader at Chicago's Rush Medical College, used mortality statistics and a then-new instrument of environmental assessment — the eudiometer — to construct environmental profiles of places Chicagoans perceived as unhealthful. Chicago's cemetery, then located where Lincoln Park is today, along the shores of Lake Michigan northwest of downtown, was perceived as particularly miasmatic. Suspecting the cemetery as a point source for the pollution of the city's potable water supply, which came from the Lake, Rauch documented shoreline currents that proceeded from the cemetery site toward the city reservoir. Finding a correlation between high water tables and rates of putrefaction in the cemetery, Rauch organized a public campaign to remove the cemetery's occupants to a 'rural' location. Although the desire to make more profitable use of urban land, esthetic fashion, as well as health concerns, drove the calculus for rural cemeteries in Boston and Philadelphia, Rauch's Chicago effort seems motivated solely by his concern for public health (Rauch 1866).

Moving the cemetery away from the Lake and settled areas would only stop the production of morbid poisons, however, and Rauch thought something additional was required to ameliorate the former cemetery ground's reservoir of miasma. His solution was to transform the cemetery grounds into a public park. The park's new plantings and engineered land forms would "detoxify" the contaminated soils and contain gases that, if emitted into the air, would prove "otherwise injurious" (Rauch 1866, 66).

Politically, Rauch faced the task of persuading civic leaders that it was wise to use substantial public sums to transform one

The dairy in
Prospect Park,1909.
PHOTO USED WITH PERMISSION
BY PROSPECT PARK ARCHIVES,
BOB LEVINE COLLECTION

area — the former cemetery — and not another. In his influential 1868 report — "Public Parks: Their Effect upon the Moral, Physical and Sanitary Conditions of the Inhabitants of Large cities; with special reference to the City of Chicago" — Rauch sought to finesse the issue with a medical rationale. Miasma, he declared, does not reside in any one community or place. Its "subtle and invisible influence may be wafted to the remotest parts, abated in virulence, but still pestiferous." In 1869, in response to the campaign Rauch led, Illinois created a multi-park system for Chicago that would surround what was then the city's perimeter. Ten years later, Rauch boasted that "at least one million" trees had been planted in Chicago and that its planned 2,500 acres of new parks would lead to "diminished mortality rates and the improved general health of all city residents" (Rauch 1879, 15).

New York and Frederick Law Olmsted

As Rauch prepared his "Public Parks" report, he became acquainted with Olmsted's approach, and the two began corresponding. By the time Rauch and Olmsted became aware of each other, the latter had a well furnished imagination concerning how to prevent disease and encourage health through environmental manipulations of various kinds. Active during the Civil War as General Secretary of the U.S. Sanitary Commission, the New York-based volunteer organization that oversaw design and support for Union military camps and field hospitals, Olmsted was familiar with medical arguments for maximizing air circulation in dwellings as well as the dangers of decay of vegetable and animal matter. He recommended that Union military hospitals be designed so that each patient received no less than 800 cubic feet of fresh air each day, for example.

For parks and early suburbs, he and Calvert Vaux, his frequent collaborator, believed, like Rauch, that if the land did not generate salubrity, then the land needed to be re-engineered so that it did. Though it may seem counterintuitive to us, who may perceive Central Park (Manhattan) and Prospect Park's (Brooklyn) landforms as preserved natural scenery, Olmsted described the Central Park project as a "transformation of a broken, rocky, sterile, and intractable body of land, more than a mile square in extent, into a public ground." (In fact, constructing Central Park was the **largest public works** project

→ SEE SUGARMAN PAGE 138

Bethesda Fountain in
Central Park, circa 1902.
PHOTO BY BENJAMIN J. FALK
USED WITH PERMISSION BY
LIBRARY OF CONGRESS PRINTS
AND PHOTOGRAPHS DIVISION

undertaken by New York City during the 19th century (Sutton 1971).

Olmsted, Vaux and their reformist contemporaries drew on an aesthetic sensibility that owed much to British and American designers of the late 18th and early 19th centuries, Capability Brown, William Kent, Humphrey Repton, and the American house designer Andrew Jackson Downing. None of these men embraced either cities or large-scale industry. Instead, their designs tended to evoke either a sanitized version of cottage life (Downing) or tidy arcadias replete with grazing livestock and sonorous rivulets (Brown and Repton). Olmsted and Vaux took cues from them. In its original version, Prospect Park, for example, contained an active dairy where visitors might purchase fresh milk, and in its first years Bethesda Fountain in Central Park provided free and clean drinking water. Prospect Park's dairy cows and the Bethesda Fountain provided vital commodities — safe milk and water — that ordinary city-dwellers of the 1860s and 1870s could not easily obtain otherwise. According to Olmsted:

> It is one great purpose of the (Central) Park to supply to the hundreds
> of thousands of tired workers, who have no opportunity to spend their
> summers in the country, a specimen of God's handiwork that shall be to
> them, inexpensively, what a month or two in the White Mountains or the
> Adirondacks is, at great cost, to those in easier circumstances
> (quoted in Sutton 1971).

Olmsted and Vaux also wanted 'natural features' in parks to promote harmony in human bodies at the individual and group levels. According to Olmsted, however, experiencing harmony was not something that one willed into being; instead, he wrote, parks had to be designed so that harmonious perceptions could arise spontaneously. How different groups of people and vehicles moved among each other was a crucial factor when considering public harmony. Careful consideration of circulatory pathways, which Olmsted pursued in a different register in his sanitary designs for military hospitals and camps, assumed great importance. He and Vaux designed separate roadways and grade changes to prevent unwanted and dangerous encounters between pedestrians, carriages, and horseback riders without having people use conscious judgment. For Olmsted, to be in one of his large urban parks was to experience "each individual adding by his mere presence to the pleasure of all others, all helping to the greater happiness of each. You may thus often see vast numbers of persons brought closely together, poor and rich, young and old, Jew and Gentile" (Sutton 1971).

Olmsted's contemporaries came to see large urban parks as among democracy's finest achievements. As Henry Bellows rhapsodized in the "Atlantic Monthly" in the late 1860s, Central Park was "the most striking evidence of the sovereignty of the people yet afforded in the history of free institutions...It is a royal work, undertaken and achieved by the Democracy — surprising equally themselves and their skeptical friends at home and abroad" (Sutton 1971, 75). When Henry James took up the "social question" of public mixing in his "The American Scene" of 1905, he observed of Central Park that "to pass...from the discipline of the streets to this so different many-smiling presence is to be thrilled at every turn" (James 1968).

Conclusion

As Meristem and others advocate for Restorative Commons of various kinds, they receive the response from skeptics that the "scientific data" is not sufficiently established to warrant the initiative. They will hear that scientific consensus is necessary before society ought to embrace a significant change or new policy. Some of this country's most successful environmental initiatives, however, have been implemented when the science was still inchoate. When Congress passed the Clean Air & Water statutes of the 1970s, for example, environmental studies were in their infancy from a modern scientific perspective. What carried the initiatives forward politically was not a settled view from the scientists, but a mix of science and public resolve that America should not continue to poison its water and air so profligately. In the 19th century, Olmsted, Rauch, and their allies were able to curry public favor not on the basis of then cutting-edge science, the germ theory that was taking form in Louis Pasteur's lab in remote Paris, but by persuading city dwellers that they could enjoy each other in large public spaces that promoted health at the individualand social levels.

The shared vocabulary of health, disease, and environmental conditions that inspired them began to wane in the 1890s. Influential physicians began abandoning miasma theory and its preoccupation with general environmental conditions in favor of laboratory models of

Olmsted's contemporaries came to see large urban parks as among democracy's finest achievements.

disease causation based on discrete species of bacteria, viruses, and parasites. If, for example, one wanted to control diphtheria, the then-new logic ran, one did not need to build a great park; instead, one should develop a mass vaccination campaign to immunize the young. Instead of going broad in their environmental manipulations, the new medical sensibility recommended going narrow.

Now, early in the 21st century, many factors favor a return to the health/environmental dualism that flowered in the middle of the 19th century, notably in the great public parks of New York City and Chicago. Meristem, along with urban leaders, has great work to do as it reinvigorates in contemporary terms an approach that has generated much pleasure and sense of well-being among city dwellers.

Literature Cited

Grob, G. 2005. The deadly truth: A history of disease in America. Cambridge, MA: Harvard University. Press. 349 p.

James, H. 1968. The American scene. Bloomington, IN: Indiana University Press. 486 p.

Pierce, B.L. 1937-57 (3 volumes). A history of Chicago. New York: Knopf.

Rauch, J. 1866. Intramural interments in populous cities and their influence upon health and epidemics. Chicago: Tribune Co.

Rauch, J. 1879. The sanitary problems of Chicago, past and present. Cambridge, MA: Riverside Press.

Sutton, S.B., ed. 1971. Civilizing American cities: a selection of Frederick Law Olmsted's writings on city landscapes. Cambridge, MA: MIT Press. 310 p.

Szczygiel, B.; Hewitt, R. 2000. Nineteenth-century medical landscapes: John H. Rauch, Frederick Law Olmsted, and the search for salubrity. Bulletin of the History of Medicine. 74(4): 708-734.

Szreter, S; Mooney, G. 1998. Urbanisation, mortality and the standard of living debate: new estimates of the expectation of life at birth in nineteenth-century British cities. Economic History Review. 50(84): 84-112.

Valencius, C.B. 2002. The health of the country: how American settlers understood themselves and their land. New York: Basic Books. 388 p.

From infancy we concentrate happily on ourselves and other organisms. We learn to distinguish life from the inanimate and move toward it like moths to a porch light....To explore and affiliate with life is a deep and complicated process in mental development. To an extent still undervalued in philosophy and religion, our existence depends on this propensity, our spirit is woven from it, hope rises on its currents.

—E.O. Wilson 1984
"Biophilia"

Biophilia, Health, and Well-being

Judith Heerwagen, Ph.D.
J.H. Heerwagen & Associates

If there is an evolutionary basis for biophilia, as asserted by E.O. Wilson in the opening quote, then contact with nature is a basic human need: not a cultural amenity, not an individual preference, but a universal primary need. Just as we need healthy food and regular exercise to flourish, we need ongoing connections with the natural world. Fortunately, our connections to nature can be provided in a multitude of ways: through gardening, walking in a park, playing in the water, watching the birds outside our window, or enjoying a bouquet of flowers.

The experience of nature across evolutionary time periods has left its mark on our minds, our behavioral patterns, and our physiological functioning. We see the ghosts of our ancestors' experiences in what we pay attention to in the environment, how we respond, and what the experience means to us. The biophilia hypothesis and supporting research tells us that, as a species, we are still powerfully responsive to nature's forms, processes, and patterns (Kellert & Wilson 1993, Kellert et al. 2008). Using knowledge of our affinity for nature, adapted and refined over millions of years, we can generate experiences of health and wellness through the environments we create. Work environments can become both more relaxed and productive, homes more harmonious, and public spaces can become more inclusive; offering a sense of belonging, security, and even celebration to a wider cross section of people.

To understand the deep underpinnings of biophilia and its manifestation in today's cultural and physical landscape, we need to go back in time to our ancestral life as mobile hunting and gathering bands. Buildings are newcomers on the evolutionary scene — a mere 6,000 or so years old. For the vast majority of human existence, the natural landscape provided the resources necessary for human survival, chief among them water, sunlight, animal and vegetable food, building materials, shelter, vistas, and fire. The sun provided warmth and light as well as information about time of day. Large trees provided shelter from the midday sun and places to sleep at night to avoid terrestrial predators. Flowers and seasonal vegetation provided food, materials, and medicinal treatments. Rivers and watering holes provided the foundation for life — water for drinking and bathing, fish and other animal resources for food. Waterways also provided a means of navigation to reach distant lands.

Our Restorative Commons:
Linking Nature to Human Health and Well-being

The Restorative Commons idea represents a significant new approach to the development of common urban spaces. Like restorative garden design, it incorporates findings from recent and interdisciplinary research on human experiences with the natural environment. The Restorative Commons approach also builds upon best practices in urban restoration ecology as well as the persistent concerns for equitable access to nature-rich environments in urban settings. Nature is beneficial to all, regardless of age, gender, race, or ethnicity and it should be available to all urban dwellers, not just those who can afford to live on the edges of parks and open spaces. Connection to nature on a daily basis reinforces the values of respect and care for the environment that are necessities for sustainable communities.

However, not all nature is equally attractive or beneficial. Spaces with dead and dying plants and trees signal habitat depletion and are largely avoided. In contrast, places with rich vegetation, flowers, large trees, water, and meandering pathways that open suddenly to views are sought out by many as places of relaxation and enjoyment. These features characterize the most beloved urban parks and arboreta across the globe. But even small spots of nature — a flower pot, tree,

Connection to nature on a daily basis reinforces the values of respect and care for the environment that are necessities for sustainable communities.

Brooklyn window box
and fire escape gardens
enrich both inside
and outside views.
PHOTO USED WITH PERMISSION
BY PHOTOGRAPHER JOHN SEITZ

or a small garden — also delight. That is the real story of our connection to nature — it has many faces and many ways to create positive experiences in our homes, offices, backyards, or common spaces. The genetic basis for biophilia does not, of course, dismiss cultural, geographic, or ecotype specificity. In fact, using inspiration from both the local natural environment and vernacular cultural expressions for creating a sense of place is critical to the success of biophilic design.

The Value of Nature to Human Health and Well-being

Improved moods and reduced stress are the most consistent benefits of nature contact across research studies, regardless of whether they are controlled laboratory experiments or field studies. Furthermore, contact with nature can be purely visual or multi-sensory, active engagement (walking, running, gardening) or passive (viewing only). Benefits are found in multiple settings, multiple cultures, and across the age span, from early childhood to late adulthood.

Although the belief in the therapeutic benefits of nature contact is ancient, the first well controlled empirical test of this hypothesis was published in 1984 by Roger Ulrich using data from a hospital setting. Ulrich tested the effect of window views on hospital patient outcomes. Half the patients had a window that looked out onto a brick wall while the others viewed an outdoor landscape with trees. All patients had the same kind of surgery, with the two different view groups matched for age, gender, and general health conditions. Ulrich found that patients with the tree view used less narcotic and milder analgesics, indicating lower pain experience. They also stayed in the hospital for a shorter time period and had a more positive post-surgical recovery overall than did patients who had the view of the brick wall.

A decade of subsequent research by Ulrich and colleagues at Texas A&M University, largely in laboratory experiments, reinforces the findings from the hospital study. Subjects exposed to a stressor recover faster and more positively if they are shown nature scenes or urban scenes with nature, rather than urban scenes devoid of natural elements. Subjects viewing the completely natural scenes do the best overall, with the greatest and most rapid reduction in physiological stress and more rapid mood enhancement. Ulrich's work has shown that nature contact can be beneficial, whether it is real or simulated. In fact, in many environments, such as windowless spaces, simulations may be the only way to create beneficial experience. A study of windowed and windowless offices by Heerwagen and Orians (1986) supports this conclusion. They found that people in windowless spaces used twice as many nature elements (posters and photos especially) to decorate their office walls than those who had window views to natural areas outdoors.

Research on nature benefits has blossomed from this early beginning to encompass a huge body of studies and findings (see Kellert et al. 2008, for an overview of biophilia research and applications). A few select benefits of nature and natural processes explored in the literature are touched on here.

SUNLIGHT

We have known for a long time that people prefer daylight environments and that they believe daylight is better for health and psychological functioning than is electric light. However, a clear delineation of the health and well-being benefits is relatively recent. We know now that bright daylight has medicinal properties. It entrains circadian rhythms, enhances mood, promotes neurological health, and affects alertness. (Figueiro et al 2002, Heerwagen 1990). Research in hospital settings shows that patients in bright rooms recover more rapidly from illness, show reduced pain levels, take fewer strong analgesics, and stay in the hospital fewer days than patients who are in more dimly lit rooms located on the north side or in locations where nearby buildings block sun penetration (Walch et al. 2005). The benefits of sunlight can be experienced in even brief walks outdoors on a sunny day or through design of spaces that integrate daylight and sun into the interior.

OUTDOOR GREEN SPACE

Research conducted in outdoor spaces expands on the benefits discovered in laboratory settings (Sullivan et al. 2004, Kweon et al. 1998). The study of **public housing projects** in Chicago by Sullivan and colleagues (2004) from the University of Illinois has found many benefits from having large trees close at hand. Using behavioral observations and interviews, the researchers found that housing developments with large trees attracted people to be outdoors and, once there, they talked to their neighbors and developed stronger

→ SEE BENNATON PAGE 232

The biophilia hypothesis tells us that, as a species, we are still powerfully responsive to nature's forms, processes, and patterns.

social bonds than people in similar housing projects without green space and trees. Furthermore, related studies found that children performing activities in green settings have shown reduced symptoms of Attention Deficit Hyperactivity Disorder (Faber et al 2001, Kuo and Faber 2004). The researchers concluded that providing "green time" for children may be an important supplement to medicine and behavioral therapies. The research from these studies supported one of the most extensive tree planting program in Chicago's history.

In another large scale urban nature project, researchers in the Netherlands are conducting a nationwide study of the benefits of green space — which they call Vitamin G — at the household, community and regional levels (Groenewegen et al. 2006). Using national health survey data arrayed on a geographical information system that shows the location of green spaces, the researchers have found preliminary evidence that residents who are closer to green spaces, including household gardens and neighborhood parks as well as large green spaces, have better health profiles than residents who are farther away. To develop these profiles, researchers used data from the Netherlands national health survey on physical and mental health and perceptions of social safety and also conducted interviews of residents living near or at a distance from green spaces. The data analysis controlled for socio-economic factors, which have known links to health outcomes. Future research will focus on identifying the mechanisms behind the relationships, particularly stress reduction, emotional restoration, physical activity, and social integration.

GARDENS AND GARDENING

There is also growing evidence that both active and passive contact with gardens provides psychological, emotional, and social benefits. In their book "Healing Gardens...", Cooper-Marcus and Barnes (1995) show that benefits of gardens include recovery from stress, having a place to escape to, and improved moods. Benefits also occur with **horticulture therapy**, especially in clinical settings and nursing homes. Other studies provide evidence that dementia and stroke patients show improved mobility and dexterity, more confidence, and improved social skills as a result of gardening activities. (Rappe 2005, Ulrich 2002). According to Ulrich, gardens will be more likely to be

→ SEE KAMP PAGE 110

Previous Page:
Washington Market Park,
Manhattan.
PHOTO USED WITH PERMISSION
BY PHOTOGRAPHER ANNE WIESEN

calming and to ameliorate stress if they contain rich foliage, flowers, a
water feature, congruent nature sounds (bird songs, moving water), and
visible wildlife, particularly birds.

Other researchers also have found improvements in emotional
functioning and reductions in stress. For instance, a laboratory study of
"green exercise" tested the effects of projected scenes on physiological
and psychological outcomes of subjects on a treadmill. They found
that all subjects benefited similarly in physiological outcomes, but that
subjects who viewed pleasant nature scenes (both rural and urban)
scored higher in measures of self-esteem than those viewing totally
urban scenes or "unpleasant" rural scenes with destroyed landscapes
(Pretty et al. 2003, 2005). Similar results have been found in field
studies by Hartig and colleagues (1991) who looked at the stress
reducing effects of walking in an urban environment with nature as
compared to a similar walk without natural elements.

NATURE AND CHILD DEVELOPMENT
The cumulative research on the benefits for children of playing in
natural environments is so compelling that it has resulted in an
outpouring of response to Richard Louv's (2005) book, "Last Child in
the Woods: Saving our Children from Nature Deficit Disorder." Playing
in outdoor environments, whether at home, school, or camp, has
sustained benefits for social, emotional, and cognitive development
in children. Nature provides both the platform and the **objects for**   → SEE STONE PAGE 122
play (Kahn and Kellert 2002). It encourages exploration and building
among older children which aids orientation and wayfinding, group
decision-making, knowledge of how to respond to changing contexts,
and improved problem-solving. Among younger children, small-scale
natural environments with props (flowers, stones, sticks, water)
stimulate imaginative play which is considered a cornerstone of social
and cognitive development.

Qualities and Attributes of Nature in Biophilic Design

Our fascination with nature is derived not just from natural elements,
but also from the qualities and attributes of natural settings that
people find particularly appealing and aesthetically pleasing. The
goal of biophilic design is to create places imbued with positive

emotional experiences — enjoyment, pleasure, interest, fascination, and wonder — that are the precursors of human attachment to and caring for place (Kellert et al. 2008). Although these biophilic design practices are not yet integrated into standards or guidelines, there is increasing interest in this topic, particularly as it relates to sustainability and social equity. We know from everyday experience that nature is not equitably distributed in urban environments. Those who can afford to do so live near parks, have large street trees and rich landscaping around their homes, and work in places that have design amenities. However, as the section below shows, there are many ways to incorporate biophilic design features throughout the **urban built fabric**. While living nature is always highly desirable, it is possible to design with the qualities and features of nature in mind, thereby creating a more naturally evocative space. Design imagination can create many pleasing options out of this biophilic template:

→ SEE BROWN PAGE 90

HERACLITEAN MOTION

Nature is always on the move. Sun, clouds, water, tree leaves, grasses — all move on their own rhythms or with the aid of wind. Katcher and Wilkins (1993) hypothesize that certain kinds of movement patterns may be associated with safety and tranquility, while others indicate danger. Movement patterns associated with safety show "Heraclitean" motion that is a soft pattern of movement that "always changes, yet always stays the same." Examples are the movement of trees or grasses in a light breeze, aquarium fish, or the pattern of light and shade created by cumulus clouds. In contrast, movement patterns indicative of danger show erratic movement and sudden change, such as changes in light and wind associated with storms, or birds fleeing from a hawk.

CHANGE AND RESILIENCE

All natural habitats show cycles of birth, death, and regeneration. Some life-like processes, such as storms and the diurnal cycle of light, also may be said to show developmental sequences. When stressed, natural spaces show remarkable signs of resilience. Yet, often in our built environments, stress leads to the onset of deterioration (e.g., vacant and abandoned buildings) that seems inevitable and incapable of renewing itself. Resilience is affected by the web of relationships that connect the composition of species within an ecological community. Waste from one animal becomes food for another; unused space becomes a niche for a newcomer; decaying trees become resources and living spaces for a variety of plants and animals. The use of recycled elements and the natural aging of materials can create this impression of resilience in built environments (Krebs 1985).

VARIATIONS ON A THEME

Natural elements — trees, flowers, animals, shells — show both variation and similarity in form and appearance due to growth patterns. Nicholas Humphrey (1980) refers to this phenomenon as "rhyming" and claims that it is the basis for aesthetic appreciation — a skill that evolved for classifying and understanding sensory experience, as well as the objects and features of the environment. He writes, "beautiful 'structures' in nature and art are those which facilitate the task of classification by presenting evidence of the taxonomic relationships between things in a way which is informative and easy to grasp."

Clematis spp. and Boston Ivy (*Parthenocissus tricuspidata*) on a Brooklyn rooftop garden display change and resilience across the seasons.
PHOTOS USED WITH PERMISSION BY PHOTOGRAPHER JOHN SEITZ

Children transform their
play environment with
found natural materials.
PHOTO USED WITH PERMISSION
BY PHOTOGRAPHER ANNE WIESEN

A closer look at
plants forms reveals
"rhyming" and
"discovered complexity".
PHOTO USED WITH PERMISSION
BY PHOTOGRAPHER JOHN SEITZ

Designers could more effectively use the principles of rhyming in a wide array of applications — in the design of circulation systems that use varied sensory conditions to reinforce wayfinding, in interior spaces with varied patterns and color, and for transitions between the outdoors and indoors.

DISCOVERED COMPLEXITY

All living organisms display complex design that may not be apparent at first glance, but is discovered through sensory exploration. The desire to know more about a space or object with increased exploration is considered by many to be at the heart of learning: the more you know, the more you want to know and the deeper the mystery becomes. In contrast to living forms and spaces, most built objects and spaces are readily knowable at first glance, and thus do not motivate learning and exploration. Although complexity is a desirable feature, spaces and objects that are too complex are difficult to comprehend. The key may be the combination of ordering and complexity that allows comprehension at higher levels first and then engages our sensory systems at a more detailed level with successive exploration (Hildebrand 1999, Kaplan and Kaplan 1989).

MULTI-SENSORY

Natural habitats are sensory rich and convey information to all human sensory systems, including sight, sound, touch, taste, and odor. Life-supporting processes, such as fire, water, and sun, also are experienced in multi-sensory ways. Many of our built environments shun sensory embellishment, creating instead caverns of grey and beige, as well as outdoor soundscapes that stress rather than soothe. Although the vast majority of research in environmental aesthetics focuses on the visual environment, there is growing interest in understanding how design appeals to multiple senses. Both the Japanese practice of "Kansei engineering" and emotion-centered design are grounded in links between sensory perception and emotional responses to artifacts and to specific features of products (McDonagh et al. 2004; also see www.designandemotion.org).

> The goal of biophilic design is to create places imbued with positive emotional experiences — enjoyment, pleasure, interest, fascination, and wonder — that are the precursors of human attachment to and caring for place.

TRANSFORMABILITY

Natural outdoor spaces appeal to children because they are
transformable and have multiple uses. As Robin Moore notes, what
children really need for play is "unused space and loose parts" (Moore
and Cooper-Marcus 2008). If given the opportunity, children will use
whatever they find in nature as play materials. Leaves, rocks, sand,
water, branches, and flowers are all used to construct and transform
an ordinary space into a magical one through imaginative play. Natural
spaces also support imaginative play more effectively than most built
structures because their features are readily transformed into different
contexts. In a study of children's play in Seattle, Kirkby (1989) found
that the most popular place on an elementary school yard was a cluster
of shrubs that children could transform into a house or a spaceship,
using flowers and twigs as play artifacts. Transformability and multi-use
are much discussed in the design world, but seldom implemented.

Reflection

This brief overview of research on biophilia and human well-being
is only the tip of a widening knowledge base that says strongly
and unequivocally that people need daily contact with the natural
environment. Fortunately, the research also shows that there is a
multiplicity of ways to ensure that people get their daily dose of "Vitamin
G." Indoor sunlight, flower pots on the doorstep, large street trees, vest
pocket parks, rooftop gardens, green roofs, large parks, water features,
views to a garden, and even positive images and representations of
nature all contribute daily perks and emotional uplifts that together
generate improved health and well-being for urban residents and for
those confined to indoor environments.

I would like to end with an anecdote from a recent talk on biophilia
to a group of designers. After discussing the emotional and physical
benefits of nature and, as a good scientist, talking about the need for
more research to clarify mechanisms and build a better business case
for biophilic design, an interior designer in the audience asked me: "Why
do we need more research? Don't we already know this? Why aren't we
putting money instead into creating these kinds of environments?"

Why, indeed? When a body of research reinforces what we know
intuitively and emotionally, isn't this really the best guide for the design?

The ideas and principles behind biophilia, built upon our understanding of human evolution in a biocentric world, enrich the design palette enormously. The biggest challenge we face is to ensure that the benefits are equitably distributed to people of all ages, abilities, and economic status. This can happen when we look at every design as an opportunity to invest in human health and well-being.

Literature Cited

Beauchemin, K.M.; Hays, P. 1996. Sunny hospital rooms expedite recovery from severe and refractory depression. Journal of Affective Disorders. 40: 49-51.

Cooper-Marcus, C.; Barnes, M.1995. Healing gardens: Therapeutic benefits and design recommendations. New York: Wiley.

Faber Taylor, A., Kuo, F.E., and Sullivan, W.C. 2001. Coping with ADD: The surprising connection to green play settings. Environment and Behavior. 33(1): 54-77

Figueiro, M.G., M.S. Rea, R.G. Stevens, and A.C. Rea. 2002. Daylight and productivity—A possible link to circadian regulation. Light and Human Health: EPRI/LRO 5th International Lighting Research Symposium: Palo Alto, CA: The Lighting Research Office of the Electric Power Research Institute: 185-193.

Groeneweggen, P.P.; van den Berg, A.E.; de Vries, S.; Verheij, R.A. 2006. Vitamin G: Effects of green space on health, well-being, and social safety. BMC Public Health. 6:149-159.

Hartig, T.; Mang, M.; Evans, G.W. 1991. Restorative effects of natural environment. Environment and Behavior. 23:3-26.

Heerwagen, J.H. 1990. Affective functioning, light hunger and room brightness preferences. Environment and Behavior. 22(5):608-635.

Heerwagen, J.H. 2006. Investing in people: The social benefits of sustainable design. Presentation at Rethinking Sustainable Construction'06; 2006 September 28-30; Sarasota, FL.

Heerwagen, J.H. 2005. The psychological value of space. Whole Building Design Guide. www.wbdg.org. (Accessed 8 July 2008.)

Heerwagen, J.H.; Orians, G.H. 1986. Adaptations to windowless: The use of visual décor in windowed and windowless offices. Environment and Behavior. 18(5): 623-629.

Heerwagen, J.H.; Orians, G.H. 1993. **Humans, habitats and aesthetics.**
In: Kellert, S.R.; Wilson, E.O., eds. The biophilia hypothesis.
Washington, DC: Island Press.

Hildebrand G (1999) **Origins of architectural pleasure.** Berkeley, CA:
University of California Press.

Humphrey, N.K. 1980. **Natural aesthetics.** In: Mikellides, B. ed.
Architecture for people. London: Studio Vista.

Kahn, P.; Kellert, S.R. 2002. **Children and nature:
Psychological, sociocultural, and evolutionary investigations.**
Cambridge, MA: MIT Press.

Kaplan, R.; Kaplan, S. 1989. **The experience of nature: A psychological
perspective.** New York: Cambridge University Press.

Katcher, A.; Wilkins,G. 1993. **Dialogue with animals: Its nature and
culture.** In: Kellert, S.R.; Wilson, E.O., eds. The biophilia hypothesis.
Washington, DC: Island Press.

Kellert, S.R.; Heerwagen, J.H.; Mador, M. 2008. **Biophilic design:
Theory, science, and practice.** New York: Wiley.

Kellert, S.R.; Wilson, E.O. 1993. **The biophilia hypothesis.** Washington,
DC: Island Press.

Kiraly, S.J.; Kiraly, M.A.; Hawe, R.D.; Makhani, N. 2006.
Vitamin D as a neuroactive substance: Review. The Scientific World
Journal. 6: 125-139.

Kirkby, M.A. 1989. **Nature as refuge in children's environments.**
Children's Environments Quarterly. 6:1-12.

Krebs, C.J. 1985. **Ecology** (3rd edition). New York: Harper & Row.

Kuo, F.E., & Faber Taylor, A. 2004. **A potential natural treatment for
Attention-Deficit/Hyperactivity Disorder: Evidence from a national
study.** American Journal of Public Health. 94(9): 1580-1586.

Kweon, B.S.; Sullivan, W.C.; Wiley, A. 1998. **Green common spaces and the
social integration of inner-city older adults.** Environment and Behavior.
30(6): 832-858.

Louv, Richard. 2005. **Last child in the woods: saving children from
nature-deficit disorder.** Chapel Hill, NC: Agonquin Books.

McDonagh, D.; Hekkert, P.; van Erp, J.; Gyi, D. 2004. **Design and
emotion.** London: Francis & Taylor.

Moore, R.C.; Cooper-Marcus, C. 2008. **Healthy planet, healthy children;
Designing nature into the daily spaces of childhood.** In: Kellert, S.R.;
Heerwagen, J.; Mador, M., eds. Biophilic design: Theory, science and
practice. New York: John Wiley & Sons.

Orians, G.H.; Heerwagen, J.H. 1992. **Evolved responses to landscapes.** In: Barkow, J.; Tooby, J.; Cosmides, L. The adapted mind. New York: Oxford University Press.

Pretty, J.; Griffin, M.; Sellens, M.; Pretty, C. 2003. **Green exercise: Complementary roles of nature, exercise, and diet in physical and emotional well-being and implications for public health policy.** CES Occasional Paper, 2003-1. Colchester, UK: Centre for Environment and Society, University of Essex.

Pretty, J.; Peacock, J.; Sellens, M.; Griffin, M. 2005. **The mental and physical Health outcomes of green exercise.** Journal of Environmental Health Research. 15(5): 319-337.

Rappe, E. 2005. **The influence of a green environment and horticultural activities on the subjective well being of the elderly living in long term care.** Publication No. 24. Finland: University of Helsinki, Department of Applied Biology.

Sullivan, W.C.; Kuo, F.E.; DePooter, S.F. 2004. **The fruit of urban nature: Vital neighborhood spaces.** Environment and Behavior. 36(5): 678-700.

Ulrich, R.S. 1993. **Biophilia and biophobia.** In: Kellert, S.R.; Wilson, E.O., eds. The biophilia hypothesis. Washington, DC: Island Press.

Ulrich, R.S. 2002. **Health benefits of gardens in hospitals.** Paper presented at Plants for People International Exhibition Foriade.

Ulrich, R.S. 1984. **View from a window may influence recovery from surgery.** Science. 224(4647): 420-421.

Walch, J.M.; Rabin, B.S; Day, R.; Williams, J.N.; Choi, K.; Kang, J.D. 2005. **The effect of sunlight on postoperative analgesic medication use: A prospective study of patients undergoing spinal surgery.** Psychosomatic Medicine. 67: 156-153.

Wilson, E.O. 1984. **Biophilia.** Cambridge, MA: Harvard University Press.

Cultivating Resilience: Urban Stewardship as a Means to Improving Health and Well-being

Erika S. Svendsen
U.S. Forest Service, Northern Research Station

Photography by **Steffi Graham**

The notion that urban open space can be a catalyst for improving human health and societal well-being is embedded throughout the history of human settlements. Public open space is part of the dynamic history of the city as it is a place of social protest and cohesion, of leisure and recreation, of exchange and use values. Yet, there are particular moments where certain characteristics of 'nature' are selectively discussed within the public discourse, thereby shaping distinct periods of urban park and open space development. These characteristics often draw upon the properties of nature that are calm, restorative, and redemptive as opposed to wild, dangerous, and disruptive.

The history of parks and open space within the American city is episodic, with distinct periods responding to a crisis, a perceived risk, or disturbance in the social order. During the **19th century**, civic and industry leaders joined forces with public health officials to support the use of parks as a way to address negative consequences of the rapidly growing industrial city. Unprecedented industrial growth created unsanitary living conditions, environmental degradation, and unsafe workplaces (Duffy 1968, Hall 1998). By the turn of the 19th century, leaders of the progressive movement were actively calling for a 'return to nature' to address the perceived moral deprivation of the poor and to better integrate them into civil society (Cranz 1982, Rosenzweig

→ SEE MARTENSEN PAGE 26

Force of Nature
Anne Adams,
Grant Avenue Community
Garden. Bronx, NY (1999)
PHOTO USED WITH PERMISSION
BY PHOTOGRAPHER STEFFI GRAHAM

and Blackmar 1992, Lawson 2005). Later, urban planners in the 1960s shifted emphasis from central and regional parks to reclaiming neighborhood open spaces in vulnerable areas as a way to promote social inclusion and urban renewal (Shiffman 1969). In the 1970s and 1980s the environmental justice movement argued that access to well maintained parks and open spaces was systematically denied to certain groups and was a visceral example of urban inequity (Francis et al. 1984, Fox et al. 1985). Reflecting on this history, one finds that in some manner or degree nearly every generation of park and open space advocacy has been driven by the pursuit and maintenance of health and well-being.

The Sustainable City

Today, urban designers, planners, and health practitioners alike are shifting from notions of the 19th century 'Sanitary City,' (Melosi 2000) to consider the 'Sustainable City,' where parks and the greater open space environs are understood as part of a larger system offering a wide range of interdependent benefits that include socioeconomic and biophysical factors (Cranz and Boland 2004, Grove, in press). These multiple benefits are important as we try to understand how urban environments, particularly parks and open spaces, contribute to the varied stages of wellness and recovery. Still, 19th century lessons regarding our health and the built environment are relevant today as populations in many parts of the world continue to become ill from typhoid and cholera while others suffer from a host of entirely new health problems such as obesity and cardiovascular disease. Ultimately, what we may discover is not only do we need innovative building design and well maintained open space but to sustain the connection to public health we need to know more about how different designs, programs, and levels of stewardship contribute to collective well-being and health.

The restorative aspect of the commons may depend, in part, upon the characteristics of place and, in part, upon us. Use and restoration of space, according to long-term research in environmental psychology, often depends on age and lifestyle as much as overall design and species composition (Kaplan and Kaplan 1989, Schroeder 1989, Dwyer et al. 1992, Lewis 1996, Gobster 2001). That is, different types of restorative spaces are required at different stages of life and the use of space depends upon personal preference. One day an individual might prefer the experience of a serene woodland walk and the next, desire the lively social experience of a community garden. Dr. Howard Frumkin suggests that sense of place is a public health construct. Frumkin writes:

> "People are heterogeneous in response to place. Some like forests, others like deserts, others like manicured back yards, and other like bustling city streets. A person's 'place in the world,' including socioeconomic status, sense of efficacy and opportunity, and cultural heritage, affects the experience of place" (Frumkin 2003:1451).

A key objective of this paper is to examine how different motivations and preferences may lead to collective modes of civic environmental stewardship such as conservation, management, monitoring, advocacy, and education. Further, how does active stewardship strengthen our resiliency at the individual, interpersonal, and community scale? Resiliency, rather than 'good health,' is considered to be a more effective indicator for measuring community well-being particularly as we grow to understand that both human and overall ecosystem health is not static but changing over time. At the same time, stewardship and the active enjoyment of urban open space may produce the type of social and spatial relationships that help us to endure stressful episodes and conditions at the societal level.

Resilience, Adaptive Capacity, and the Non-equilibrium Paradigm

Derived from its Latin roots, the meaning of resilience is literally 'to jump or leap back' to some earlier state of being. We often marvel at instances of nature's resilient return after damage from fire, flood, or wind. At the same time, we praise the ability of our own species to recover from misfortunes brought about by a change in health, social status, or financial security. The notion of restoring any system to a prior point of existence following a disturbance or traumatic experience is misleading. Instead, we find ourselves, as well as our environments, to exist as part of a dynamic continuum. Urban ecologists refer to this dynamic as the non-equilibrium paradigm (McDonnell and Pickett 1993). Despite all our technological achievements, humans — along with all the other species on Earth — ultimately coexist within a murky world of feast and famine, triumphs and failures, good days and bad. However, there is hope to

How does active stewardship strengthen our resiliency at the individual, interpersonal, and community scale?

Battleground
Trash-strewn Lot,
Eagle Avenue.
Bronx, NY (1999)
PHOTO USED WITH PERMISSION
BY PHOTOGRAPHER STEFFI GRAHAM

*Phoenix Rises
on Eagle Avenue*
Dimas Cepeda,
El Batey Borincano.
Bronx, NY (1999)
PHOTO USED WITH PERMISSION
BY PHOTOGRAPHER STEFFI GRAHAM

mitigate our misfortunes as theories, methods, and tools have been developed to deepen our understanding of the beneficial link between human health and the environment. For example, a key component to our individual and collective pursuit for a healthy society and ecosystem function is what many fields of science refer to as an 'adaptive capacity' (Olsson et al. 2004). Or, in other words, how well do we adapt to change? The more resilient we are the more likely we are to successfully adapt to the changes inherent in a dynamic system. How well we manage to adapt, both plants and people alike, depends upon a wide range of social and biophysical factors. Our likelihood for improved health and well-being depends upon our past histories but also our current and future situations in life. Recovery from an illness, similar to recovery of ecosystem functions, often depends upon what public health researchers refer to as the '*life course*' (Ben-Shlomo and Kuh 2002) and what urban ecologists have termed '*subtle human effects*' (McDonnell and Pickett 1993). The life course approach focuses on the long-term effects of physical and social exposures through the course of one's life — from gestation to old age. It considers the biological, behavioral, and psycho-social pathways that have the potential to impact one's health over time. Similarly, the ecological approach considers *historical effects*, which are essentially biological legacies of a particular system; *lagged effects*, which are the result of some past event; and *unexpected actions at a distance*, which are impacts far from the initial action or event (pollution impacts are a prime example). (McDonnell and Pickett 1993, Pickett et al. 1997). Together, if we consider the life course and subtle human effects approaches we begin to understand that the resilience and adaptation of our species are important not as a singular event, but as multiple and multidimensional events over time and space.

Open Space: A Dynamic and Resilient Resource

Urban systems are, of course, very complex. Northridge et al. (2003) suggest a model of this complex system with four interacting levels: a *fundamental*, macro level including the natural environment and highest level social factors like economic structure; an *intermediate* level of the built environment and social context; a *proximate* level at the interpersonal level; and finally the scale of *health and well-being* (Fig. 1). Urban planners and designers often work at the nexus of the more intermediate factors of the built environment and social systems (i.e. land use, transportation, environmental policies) while public health professionals delve into more proximate factors that include stressors such as financial insecurity, environmental toxins and unfair treatment as well as health behaviors (i.e. dietary practices, physical activity). Through this model we can see the relationships between open space and well-being as part of this systems approach. This interdisciplinary framework emphasizes the intermediate domain of the urban natural resource planner (i.e. the built environment), the proximate domain of the public health practitioner (i.e. social stressors) as critical components in improving individual-collective health and well-being. Viewed this way, we can begin to understand how public goods such as parks and open spaces are critical resources that can negatively or positively impact proximate levels of stressors, enable or discourage certain behaviors, and become mediating spaces that affect social integration.

However, the provision of physical space is only part of the story. Provision of open space is necessary, but not sufficient, to provide *restorative* environments. Design, stewardship, and engagement with open space can enhance the restorative elements open spaces can offer. This paper will present findings that focus on one aspect of this experience of place: active stewardship. Active stewardship can include a wide range of human interactions, ranging from membership and decision-making to active, hands-on work in a place. The difference between more passive forms of engagement and active stewardship is that the former explains a particular state of being while the latter indicates a level of responsibility, rights, and preferences within an interdependent system. Theoretically we are all stewards of the earth. Active stewardship is one way for us to contribute and find individual and civic meaning within this larger system (Burch and Grove 1993). For example, studies of environmental volunteers find that stewardship activities help to lessen feelings of isolation and disempowerment that can lead to depression and anxiety (Sommer et al. 1994, Svendsen and Campbell 2006, Townsend 2006). Many of these studies are based on single work days or during specific or extreme periods of crisis. In 2003, the notion of whether there might be a longer-term connection between stewardship and well-being was put to the test as part of a citywide

I. FUNDAMENTAL
macro level

II. INTERMEDIATE
meso/community level

Natural Environment
topography, climate, water supply

Built Environment

• land use
  industrial, residential; mixed use or single use

• transportation systems

• services
  shopping, banking, health care facilities, waste transfer stations

• public resources
  parks, museums, libraries

• zoning regulations

• buildings
  housing, schools, workplaces

Macrosocial Factors

• historical conditions

• political orders

• economic order

• legal codes

• human rights doctrines

• social and cultural institutions

• ideologies
  racism, social justice, democracy

Inequalities

• distribution of material wealth

• distribution of employment opportunities

• distribution of educational opportunities

• distribution of political influence

Social Context

• community investment
  economic development, maintenance, police services

• policies
  public, fiscal, environment, workspace

• enforcement of ordinances
  public, environmental, workplace

• community capacity

• civic participation and political influence

• quality of education

Figure 1
Northridge et al. (2003)
urban systems model.
Public goods such as
parks and open spaces
are critical resources
that can negatively or
positively impact proximate
levels of stressors, enable
or discourage certain
behaviors, and become
mediating spaces that
affect social integration.

III. PROXIMATE

micro/interpersonal level

IV. HEALTH & WELL-BEING

individual or population levels

Stressors

- environmental, neighborhood,

  workplace and housing conditions

- violent crime and safety

- police response

- financial insecurity

- environmental toxins
  lead, particulates

- unfair treatment

Health Outcomes

- infant and child health
  low birth weight, lead poisioning

- obesity

- diabetes

- cancers

- injuries and violence

- infectious diseases

- respiratory health
  asthma

- mental health

- all-cause mortality

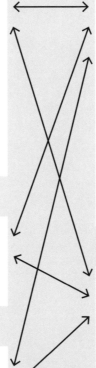

Health behaviors

- dietary practices

- physical activity

- health screening

Well-being

- hope/despair

- life satisfaction

- psychosocial distress

- happiness

- disability

- body size and body

Social Integration and Social Support

- social participation and integration

- shape of social networks and

  resources available

- social support

Feeding the World
Gardener's name unknown.
Harding Park
Beautification Project.
Bronx, NY (1999)
PHOTO USED WITH PERMISSION
BY PHOTOGRAPHER STEFFI GRAHAM

assessment of over 300 community garden groups — 23 percent of which were in existence for 21-30 years and 36 percent for 11-20 years (Svendsen and Stone 2003). The assessment was conducted through the New York City's Parks and Recreation's GreenThumb Program in partnership with the U.S. Forest Service, Northern Research Station's Urban Field Station in New York City. These findings along with city-wide study on stewardship groups are discussed here in support of a theoretical framework for active stewardship, social networks, and well-being.

The GreenThumb Study:
Understanding Individuals' Motivations for Gardening

→ SEE STONE PAGE 122

The **GreenThumb** program was established in 1978 to assist emergent community groups in reclaiming vacant, derelict space into neighborhood gardens. By the early 1990s, over 700 GreenThumb community gardens flourished in New York City neighborhoods serving thousands of residents and visitors daily. In the late 1990s, the Giuliani mayoral administration attempted to restrict the capacity of the GreenThumb program by transferring it from the Department of Parks and Recreation to the Department of Housing Preservation and Development in the hopes that the current land use would eventually be converted from gardens to housing as part of the administration's neighborhood development strategy. At the same time, the administration prepared hundreds of gardens for sale through the city's public land auction (Englander 2001). Gardeners, along with greening organizations, private foundations and the general public, joined together to protest these sales. New York City found itself in court over the garden preservation issue and in 2002, a State Attorney General-initiated lawsuit on behalf of the gardens was settled, ensuring the rights of citizen garden stewards and the preservation of the majority of gardens as public parkland or private land trusts. During this time of crisis, it was thought important to capture original participants' motivations for community gardening: what impulses were connecting these stewards to their sites such that they would advocate vigilantly to protect them? Each garden group identified a representative to participate in the assessment. The assessment was conducted by a parks staff person in a structured interview setting within the public

offices of GreenThumb. Eighty-four percent of respondents cited
the need to 'beautify the neighborhood' as a primary motivation for
founding their particular community garden. Sixty-three percent
identified with the need to 'create/improve green space' and to 'create
a place of relaxation and peace.' Forty percent recalled the need to
'provide food' or for 'economic development.' These findings suggest a
motivational purpose tied to self yet that motivation ultimately becomes
much greater than self. This subtle meaning links the individual to
the collective as both become embodied in public spaces that are
restorative. Further evidence of this can be found in the way that
gardeners talk about their motivations for active stewardship

The Language of Health and Well-being

Individual respondents to the question of 'why garden?' echoed each
other's statements through the repetition of words such as beauty,
identity, memory, food, clean, safe, education, youth, work, outdoors,
satisfaction, peace, and therapy. These words were constantly chosen
to counter words such as violence, trash, crime, drugs, and stress. A
few key quotes are selected below to illustrate this connection between
individual well-being, stewardship, and the built environment.

    Often the same space can offer different restorative qualities for
each individual. For example:

> "Cookie works for the garden because she cares about the community space.
> Miguel gardens because he wants to plant food to help feed people and to
> grow food for his family."

> "Mr. Martinez likes the garden as a place for social activities. Mr. Estrada
> likes to garden because it is like a dream, he wants to create a garden like
> no other in the city.

Garden stewardship is an experience that uniquely engages all the
senses and aids in helping individuals to relax.

> "It's like a therapy and it keeps your mind off of things."

> "It's the quiet, the green, the work itself"

> "It gives me peace of mind. I can leave my house and go sit in the garden:
> it's so peaceful to smell the air. It relieves stress and takes a whole lot of
> problems away."

Life Between the
Brooklyn Buildings
Walter Faison,
Warwick Street Greenery
Glow Garden.
Brooklyn, NY (1999)
PHOTO USED WITH PERMISSION
BY PHOTOGRAPHER STEFFI GRAHAM

Gardeners, quoted below, often respond that being an active steward in the garden helps mitigate the stress associated with transitions such as moving to a new place, growing older, and death.

"I was a gardener at home in Puerto Rico and when I moved to New York I was shocked by the lack of greenery. I had to become a gardener here. It's part of my life."

"Most of us are from the south, and we miss working with our hands"

"It's a wonderful resource for the community and for many immigrants who found it to be a relaxing and peaceful place."

"Besides beautification, it gives me something to do. I'm a retired man. I don't have time to complain about aches and pains."

"The garden helps me to relax. Also it reminds me of my mother. She helped to start this garden 25 years ago. Working the soil and seeding keeps me centered."

Gardeners report a high degree of personal satisfaction associated with gardening as a hobby but they also derive satisfaction as they see their efforts to be an important part of neighborhood resilience. Recall that the gardens emerged during a time of crisis when government services were severely cut, businesses and residents were moving out, and crime rates skyrocketed:

"Years ago our community was full of drugs and prostitution, and the community needed a strong group to fight for the right of our space. The corner of the block was empty and full of rats. We started the garden to clean the area and for safety reasons. This is what motivated us to create this beautiful garden."

"We were motivated to beautify our neighborhood, to create a place of relaxation and peace and to create a safe place of environmental restoration to escape from the negative elements like all the drug dealers. On the abandoned lot we found dead human bodies, dead animals, and garbage on it."

"It's the overall achievement that a change has been made in our community"

"I like to see things grow. Everything comes down to quality of life—clean air, local schools—we try to make it look like Central Park for the kids as they walk to school"

Stewardship in this context helped to re-establish trust, social networks and efficacy among neighbors essential for strengthening social cohesion, resiliency, and maintaining a sense of community well-being:

> "We enjoy being in the park and giving something back to others in our community. Sometimes people just come and have lunch—that's such a gift. Soon the schools will be back in session and they come in. It's helped to beautify this community."

> "With respect for each other we created this place together. Now we take care of the garden and have fun with the kids. They can learn about the pleasure of having a place and being together."

> "It's like home, it's everyone's backyard."

Based on this understanding, we find that the reciprocity that exists between individuals and their environments through pubic stewardship is tangible, visible, and not at all abstract. While stewardship is commonly triggered by a personal need or desire, the outcome often benefits both the person as well as a greater collective.

Satisfaction and accomplishment often leads to a sustained positive outlook and the *personal self-confidence* essential for taking proactive measures to care about one's health. In the context of the devastated urban landscapes of the 1970s and 1980s, neighbors regained a sense of control through greening open spaces. This act of stewardship was intimately tied to addressing the psycho-social and biophysical impact of abandoned streets as well as an individual need for control in one's own life and surroundings. "Control" here refers to the fundamental need humans have to create change in the environment and their lives rather than to *maintain control* over them. Gardens became important *expressions of self as well as community.*

Hence, the diversity of community garden design functions in New York City suggests that gardening is not only defined by the active growing of fruits, vegetables, and flowers but also is infused with issues of identity, economy and efficacy. This sense of individual-collective agency has a unique ability to tie together the built environment and larger social context with very proximate levels of human stressors, behaviors, and social integration. While the degree and type of stewardship may vary according to people and place ultimately, involvement with space is a non-passive act fundamental to activating a collective resilience inherent in both humans and the landscape. Another critical public health and well-being aspect that emerges from the motivational evidence is that stewardship enables us to *share knowledge and leave a legacy*. This research on the role of legacy and collective memory as expressed in the landscape is further explored through the **Living Memorials Project**.

→ SEE CAMPBELL PAGE 188

Many of the gardeners cited the need to teach and leave a legacy for children—and to create a physical space that could motivate and inspire others in their community overtime. As a result, gardeners take great pride in their work and often receive positive public acknowledgement for their efforts. A critical aspect of human resilience and well-being is a personal outlook tied to the notion that our individual lives are important and that they contribute to a continuum of life. Active stewardship—whether it is out on the Great Plains or on an urban street corner—is an act of great public service. Stewardship satisfies a fundamental human need to matter.

STEW-MAP:
Understanding Organizational Motivations for Stewardship

Evidence of the need for restorative actions, to share knowledge, to leave a legacy, and to establish social bonds can also be found in the density of urban environmental civic groups in New York City. STEW-MAP is the Stewardship Mapping and Assessment Project of the U.S. Forest Service, Northern Research Station's Urban Field Station in New York City in cooperation with Columbia University's Department of Sociology and the University of Vermont Spatial Analysis Lab. In 2007, working with citywide environmental groups, we developed a sample of

→ SEE MAP PAGE 18

2,793 **civic stewardship groups** (Svendsen et al. 2008). These groups were assessed in terms of their organizational structure, capacities, networks, and stewardship geographies. Many of these groups use similar restorative language such as *to strengthen*, *to improve*, *to create*, *to reclaim, and to connect* as part of describing the mission of their stewardship activities. An overwhelming amount of these groups stated that they became active environmental stewards as part of a larger organizational focus area summarized as "community improvement and capacity building." In other words, the notion of the environment and stewardship is embedded within organizations rather then being the sole function or purpose.

The majority of groups studied began as small groups of friends or neighbors who formalized their organizational structure and capacity over time. These groups now typically work within a network of other organizations, some of which are embedded within their neighborhoods, and others that connect across the city and beyond. In this sense, urban stewardship as a form of social organization may help to re-establish critical *social networks* historically disrupted by shifts in neighborhood demographics and changes in the built environment. Social networks, especially those that help to bridge spatial divides, can lead directly to community development and well-being opportunities through improved access to resources such as information, education, and multicultural experiences (Altschuler et al. 2004). At the same time, spaces that involve people in design, maintenance, use, or stewardship may foster the type of local community cohesion critical for defending against periods of economic hardship, rising crime and debris and even neighborhood stereotyping (Sampson et al. 1997). Communities with these types of dense social networks are thought to have a greater ability to adapt to change and endure during episodic incidents of stress (Klinenberg 2002). Long-term human ecology studies from Chicago (Sampson and Raudenbush 1999, Sampson 2003) have found that stewardship spaces such as community gardens are precisely the type of intervention that can make a significant difference in the public health outcomes of a given neighborhood because they have the capacity to impact the intermediate level or built environment and social context as well as proximate level social stressors such as housing conditions, unfair treatment, poor diet, or financial insecurity.

Exploration and understanding of neighborhood health geographies, access to resources and networks has become enlivened through recent writing from the field of public health (Link and Phelan 1995, Kawachi and Berkman 2003, Macintyre and Ellaway 2003, Andrews and Kearns 2005). While social networks are import catalysts for building up social capital, urban planning and more recent public health research raises a key point that all social networks are not necessarily helpful (i.e., drug and crime networks, obesity) and that what is needed in certain

Cultivating Resilience
Jim Williams,
Red Gate Garden.
Brooklyn, NY (1999)
PHOTO USED WITH PERMISSION
BY PHOTOGRAPHER STEFFI GRAHAM

The reciprocity between 'nature' and humans happens within one system as the land that we steward—no matter how small— becomes part of a biological legacy and a social legacy, strengthening our collective identity and social cohesion.

instances is different networks of information and experience that are often exogenous to a particular community (Kelly 1994, Marcuse 2000, Christakis and Fowler 2007, Christakis and Fowler 2008). A critical question emerging from the STEW-MAP evidence is whether New York City-based stewardship groups and individuals operate in trans-neighborhood networks that may help to *sustain* critical resources such as capital, materials, knowledge, and power *in situ*. This may enhance our understanding of these places from having limited environmental and social benefits to being integral to sustaining our collective resilience, efficacy and well-being within a much broader spectrum of time and place.

Conclusion: Sustaining the Restorative Commons

The reciprocity between 'nature' and humans happens within one system as the land that we steward—no matter how small—becomes part of both a biological legacy, contributing in some measure to cleaner air and water, wildlife habitats, and healthy soil as well as a social legacy, strengthening our collective identity and social cohesion. Urbanization creates diverse, dynamic and emergent landscapes (Jacobs 1961, Clay 1973, Johnson 2001). Urban open spaces in all their manifestations (e.g., parks, gardens, green roofs, urban farms, greenways) exist within a public sphere of social norms, laws, and property rights. This dynamic and heterogeneous landscape is influenced by both biophysical and ecological drivers on the one hand and social and economic drivers on the other. While design and technology can help to knit together this landscape, it is our social structure that will most likely sustain it (Spaargaren and Mol 1992). Social ecologist William R. Burch, Jr. wrote at a critical time in the 1970s environmental movement, "... our encounter with history seems special only because we look at our awesome machines and ignore our even more awesome social organizations" (Burch 1971). This is particularly salient to the pursuit of the Sustainable City. *Green* and *restorative* urban designs become sustainable solutions only when they are complimented by a self-organizing human or social system of stewardship. Or in other words, when they matter to people.

From the story of community gardeners and other civic groups in New York City, one learns how urban stewardship can be both an act of personal recovery and mechanism for maintaining individual well-being as well as a way to strengthen community efficacy and cohesion. It is suggested here that stewardship may contribute to resiliency and a positive health outlook as active stewardship builds confidence, strengthens social ties, broadens social networks, and provides the steward (or group of stewards) with social status as a positive contributor to society. This type of resiliency can have a community-wide impact. However, these benefits can be difficult to quantify or understand from the general purview of some policy and decision-makers. Too often it is not until these spaces are threatened by competing development (as in the case of community gardens in New York City), or our desired use of them is restricted, that we come to understand the full weight of their societal meaning. It is only then that we begin to understand that the true value of open space is as part of our larger collective health and well-being.

Policy-makers, designers, and planners interested in cultivating resiliency may want to consider first the most vulnerable populations and seek to recapture the flow of critical resources within these communities. It is the most vulnerable that have fewer material resources available and in some cases the type of social networks to adapt to change and challenge adversity. At the same time, we need not only to celebrate city life and difference but also to design social systems that can support and nurture a heterogeneous system of open space over time. This includes recognition of emergent open spaces and a pro-active cultivation of civic stewardship during times of crisis and change. For it is stewardship and engagement that can deepen social meaning to ensure that the Restorative Commons will be a resource that not only exists but persists through the life course. While it may be impossible to know the full extent of how local acts of stewardship have inspired others, I am reminded of a particularly evocative quote from my multi-city research:

> "It's simple. I do it [garden] so the kids around here see me taking care of things. When I'm gone or they're grown, they might remember...."
> Ms. Shirley Boyd. Franklin Square Neighborhood. Baltimore, MD
> (Svendsen and Graham 1997)

Within the history of the city one can find evidence of individuals and groups not only creating restorative spaces as part of their own desire for health and well-being but with the hope that it might also trigger resilient processes in others and benefit a larger commons.

Literature Cited

Altschuler, A.; Somkin, C.P.; et al. 2004. Local services and amenities, neighborhood social capital, and health. Social Science and Medicine. 59: 1219-1229.

Andrews, G.J.; Kearns, R.A. 2005. Everyday health histories and the making of place. Social Science and Medicine. 60: 2697-2713.

Ben-Shlomo, Y.; Kuh, D. 2002. A life course approach to chronic disease epidemiology: conceptual models, empirical challenges, and interdisciplinary perspectives. International Journal of Epidemiology. 31: 285-293.

Burch, W.R., Jr. 1971. Daydreams and nightmares—A sociological essay on the American environment. New York: Harper & Row.

Burch, W.R., Jr.; Grove, J.M. 1993. People, trees and participation on the urban frontier. Unasylva. 44: 19-27.

Christakis, N.A.; Fowler, J.H. 2007. The spread of obesity in a large social network. New England Journal of Medicine. 357: 370-9.

Christakis, N.A.; Fowler, J.H. 2008. The collective dynamics of smoking in a large social network. New England Journal of Medicine. 358: 2249-58.

Clay, G. 1973. Close up: How to read the American city. New York: Praeger Publishers.

Cranz, G. 1982. The politics of park design: A history of urban parks in America. Cambridge, MA: MIT Press.

Cranz, G.; Boland, M. 2004. Defining the sustainable park: A fifth model for urban parks. Landscape Journal. 23(2): 102-120.

Duffy, J. 1968. History of public health in New York City, 1625-1866. New York, NY: Russell Sage Foundation.

Dwyer, J.F.; Schroeder, H.W.; Gobster, P.H. 1992. The significance of urban trees and forests: Toward a deeper understanding of value. Journal of Arboriculture. 10(7): 276-284.

Englander, D. 2001. New York City gardens: A resource at risk. New York, NY: Trust for Public Land. 28 p.

Fox, T.; Koeppel, I.; Kellam, S. 1985. Struggle for space: The greening of New York City, 1970-1984. New York, NY: Neighborhood Open Space Coalition.

Francis, M.; Cashdan, L.; Paxson, L. 1984. Common open spaces: Greening neighborhoods through community action and land conservation. Washington, DC: Island Press.

Frumkin, H. 2003. Healthy places: Exploring the evidence. American Journal of Public Health. 93(9): 1451-1454.

Gobster, P.H. 2001. Visions of nature: conflict and compatibility in urban park restoration. Landscape and Urban Planning. 56: 35-51.

Grove, J.M. In press. Cities: Managing densely settled social-ecological systems. In: Chapin, F. S., III; Kofinas, G.P.; Folke, C., eds. Principles of ecosystem stewardship: Resilience-based natural resource management in a changing world. New York, NY: Springer-Verlag.

Hall, P. 1998. Cities of tomorrow: An intellectual history of urban planning and design in the twentieth century. London: UK, Blackwell Publishers.

Jacobs, J. 1961. The death and life of great American cities. New York, NY: Random House.

Johnson, S. 2001. Emergence: the connected lives of ants, brains, cities and software. New York, NY: Scribner.

Kaplan, R.; Kaplan, S. 1989. The experience of nature: A psychological perspective. Cambridge, UK: Cambridge University Press.

Kawachi, I.; Berkman, L.F., eds. 2003. Neighborhoods and health. Oxford, UK: Oxford University Press.

Kelly, M.P.F. 1994. Towanda's triumph: social and cultural capital in transition to adulthood in the urban ghetto. International Journal of Urban and Regional Research. March: 89-111.

Klinenberg, E. 2002. Heat wave: A social autopsy of disaster in Chicago. Chicago: University of Chicago Press.

Lawson, L.J. 2005. City bountiful: a century of community gardening in America. Berkeley, CA: University of California Press.

Lewis, C.A. 1996. Green nature/human nature: The meaning of plants in our lives. Champaign, IL: University of Illinois Press.

Link, B.G.; Phelan, J.C. 1995. Social conditions as fundamental causes of disease. Journal of Health and Social Behavior. 85: 80-94.

Macintyre, S.; Ellaway, A. 2003. Neighborhoods and health: An overview. In: Kawachi, I; Berkman, L, eds. Neighborhoods and health. Oxford, UK: Oxford University Press: 20-45.

Marcuse, P. 2000. Federal urban programs as multicultural planning: The empowerment zone approach. In: Burayidi, M.A., ed. Urban planning in a multicultural society. Westport, CA: Praeger: 225-233.

McDonnell, M.; Pickett, S.T.A. 1993. Humans as components of ecosystems: The ecology of subtle human effects and populated areas. New York, NY: Springer-Verlag.

Melosi, M.V. 2000. The sanitary city: urban infrastructure in America from colonial times to the present. Baltimore, MD: Johns Hopkins University Press.

Northridge, M.; Sclar, E.; et al. 2003. Sorting out the connections between the built environment and health: A conceptual framework for navigating pathways and planning healthy cities. Journal of Urban Health. 80(4): 556-568.

Olsson, P.; Folke, C.; Berkes, F. 2004. Adaptive co-management for building resilience in social-ecological systems. Environmental Management. 34(1): 75-90.

Pickett, S.T.A.; Burch, W. R., Jr.; Dalton, S. E.; Foresman, T.W.; Grove, J.M.; Rowntree, R. 1997. A conceptual framework for the human ecosystems in urban areas. Urban Ecosystem. 1: 185-199.

Rosenzweig, R.; Blackmar. E. 1992. The park and the people: A social history of Central Park. New York, NY: Cornell University Press.

Sampson, R.J. 2003. Neighborhood-level context and health: Lessons from sociology. In: Kawachi, I.; Berkman, L.F., eds. Neighborhoods and health. Oxford, UK: Oxford University Press.

Sampson, R.J.; Raudenbush, S.W. 1999. Systematic social observation of public spaces: A new look at disorder in urban neighborhoods. American Journal of Sociology. 105(3): 603-651.

Sampson, R.J.; Raudenbush, S.W., et al. 1997. Neighborhoods and violent crime: A multi-level study of collective efficacy. Science. 277: 918-924.

Schroeder, H.W. 1989. **Environment, behavior and design research on urban forests.** In: Zube, E.H.; Moore, G.T., eds. Advances in environment, behavior and design. Vol 2. New York, NY: Plenum Press.

Shiffman, R. 1969. **The Vest-pocket park as an instrument of social change.** In: Seymour, W.N., Jr. Small urban spaces: The philosophy, design, sociology and politics of vest pocket parks and other small urban open spaces. New York, NY: NYU Press.

Sommer, R.; Learey, F.; Summitt, J.; Tirrell, M. 1994. **Social benefits of residential involvement in tree planting: comparison with developer planted trees.** Journal of Arboriculture. 20(6): 323-328.

Spaargaren, G.; Mol, A.P.J. 1992. **Sociology, environment and modernity: ecological modernization as a theory of social change.** Society and Natural Resources. 5: 323-344.

Svendsen, E.; Graham, S. 1997. **Personal communication with Ms. Shirley Boyd, Franklin Square gardener.** Baltimore, MD.

Svendsen, E.; Stone, E. 2003. **New York City Parks & Recreation GreenThumb Garden Assessment Report.** City of New York Department of Recreation & Parks.

Svendsen, E.; Campbell, L. 2006. **Land-markings: 12 journeys through 9/11 living memorials.** NRS-INF-1-06. Newtown Square, PA: U.S. Department of Agriculture, Forest Service, Northern Research Station.

Svendsen, E.; Campbell, L.; Fisher, D. 2008. **Understanding urban environmental stewardship in New York City.** In: Proceedings of the international symposium on society and resource management (ISSRM): Past and future; 2008 June 10-14; Burlington, VT. Burlington, VT: University of Vermont. Abstract.

Townsend, M. 2006. **Feel blue, touch green: Participation in forest/ woodland management as a treatment for depression.** Urban Forestry and Urban Greening. 5: 111-120.

Thought Pieces

These brief pieces offer the reflections of architects on
the development of restorative green infrastructure. They
are points of entry for those unfamiliar with green building
and green infrastructure, offering an overview of the intent,
impact, and importance of this movement in the design
and building fields. They call attention to the legacy of
early innovators from the worlds of art and activism. Going
forward, they encourage us to utilize systems thinking in
the retrofitting and development of our built environment,
rights-of-way, and urban public spaces.

Re-Naturing the City: A Role for Sustainable Infrastructure and Buildings

Hillary Brown, FAIA
New Civic Works

Design professionals and planners are learning new ways to weave nature into the urban experience through the vehicle of high performance or green building. With energy- and resource-efficient building practices joined to metrics such as air quality, indoor lighting, and thermal comfort, environmental quality is being expressly redefined by better human outcomes. Put back in touch with daylight's full spectrum, embracing the lost logic of passive solar heating and natural ventilation, reconnecting with the world outside, enjoying designs that promote views for everyone to experience weather, seasons, and views, we may once again benefit from proximity to the natural world.

Sustainability, many are coming to understand, is not about austerity, but to the contrary, may proffer a richer, more sensuous experiential dimension. Practiced well, it's about keeping abundant the **visual, tactile, acoustic, and thermal cues** that are our link to natural processes. Locked in conventionally lit, hard-surfaced, climate-controlled interiors, with ever more social and business transactions being mediated electronically, human senses can wither. They become anaesthetized. Green design privileges access by all of our faculties to daylight, views, and fresh air, enabling us to feel or hear sound of wind or water, providing the "thermal delight" experienced indoors in a sunny spot or outdoors on a green roof. Vegetated roofscapes and rain gardens bring nature close to hand while beneficially catching, cleaning, or even infiltrating stormwater right on site. In sum, buildings that celebrate local microclimate, topology, vegetation, hydrology, and material

→ SEE HEERWAGEN PAGE 38

Previous Page:
Street tree and skyline, Brooklyn, NY.
PHOTO USED WITH PERMISSION BY PHOTOGRAPHER IAN CHENEY

Left:
The West Side Highway looking north from the pedestrian bridge at Rector Street. Planted medians buffer adjacent pedestrian and bicycle pathways from highway car traffic and provide welcome views.
PHOTO USED WITH PERMISSION BY PHOTOGRAPHER ANNE WIESEN

Green roof on Chicago's City Hall.
PHOTO BY LINDSAY CAMPBELL,
U.S. FOREST SERVICE

Green infrastructure and redesigned streetscape improve bicycle and pedestrian transportation.
PHOTO USED WITH PERMISSION
BY NEW YORK CITY DEPARTMENT
OF TRANSPORTATION

Front yard urban tree
canopy in Carroll Gardens,
Brooklyn.
PHOTO USED WITH PERMISSION
BY PHOTOGRAPHER IAN CHENEY

resources, may realize both greater efficiency and effectiveness, being more comfortable and conducive to productivity, than conventional buildings that ignore their surroundings.

The techniques and resultant benefits of closely coupling built and natural systems described above can today be applied to the design and construction of the public right-of-way — that familiar urban cross-section of sidewalk, street trees, parking and travel lanes, and associated subsurface utility and stormwater infrastructures. Indeed, the right-of-way remains today a typology of the "commons" and is, in fact, an undervalued public space that can offer significant ecological and human health benefits. Our city streets can move toward high performance by application of the core principles of sustainable design — using materials, energy, and resources more effectively, limiting hazardous substances and waste, and reducing other detrimental impacts to the air, water, and soil.

Best practices for the right-of-way marry nature's economy of means to her beneficial processes. A few examples may illuminate this point. **Treating stormwater runoff** as close to its source as possible by using landscaped or "bioengineered" structures in roadway medians or in sidewalk areas can return cleaner water to its natural hydrologic pathways. In lieu of the conventional, miserly 5 ft x 5 ft tree pit, trees may be connected continuously under the sidewalk pavement with continuous trenches filled with structural soil (organic matter mixed in a matrix of large stones). This allows trees' roots air and room for growth, while providing a useful stormwater reservoir. Through shading and evaporation, trees combat the local "heat island effect" of higher summertime city temperatures while reducing heat stress on asphalt pavement. So can light-colored asphalt and concrete on streets and sidewalks that deflect some incoming solar gain. At night the city also benefits from pavement's greater reflectivity as it boosts the effectiveness of streetlight illumination. Diversified native (water efficient) plant and tree species, brought in greater density to our streetscapes, enhance the walkability of the right-of-way — improving public health, safety, and quality of life.

Envision, if you will, such a transformation of New York City's largest real estate holding, namely its 20,000 lane- miles of right-of-way — an aggregate area greater than the island of Manhattan. By combining

→ SEE LACERTE PAGE 216

→ SEE MARSHALL AND HODA
  PAGE 164

these progressive "best practices" across landscape architecture, civil engineering, and utility conveyance systems, the rights-of-way become a whole system, an integration of many parts combined for their higher performance in a densely urbanized environment. By incorporating into engineered systems the intelligence of natural ones, whose passive processes clean and cool air and water (using infiltration, bio-retention, bio-remediation and evapo-transpiration), and by helping to replenish and augment plant species health and diversity, utilitarian public works can begin to transcend their single purpose functions. This gentle 'greening of gray infrastructure' can also, over long time horizons, achieve a subtle but profound re-naturing of the city. Locally and nationally, as we proceed with a new era of infrastructure upgrade, our goal should be to make this relatively taken-for-granted real estate more resilient, functional, and beautiful, fostering a healthier urban environment.

Overcoming our increasingly devastating disconnect from the natural world has permitted us to accept as norms the terms of pollution, sprawl, social isolation and a generalized diminishment in human experience and potential. Re-energizing our symbiotic relationship with nature in an urbanizing landscape is perhaps one of the most pressing needs and potent opportunities of our time.

Utilitarian public works can begin to transcend their single purpose functions.

Urban Gardens: Catalysts for Restorative Commons Infrastructure

John M. Seitz, AIA
HOK

Nature continues to define the restorative landscape. While our early commons, a central shared field for grazing or crops, has changed over the centuries, our urban infrastructure is a new necessity that has paralleled the growth of cities and that carries with it remnant functions of these commons. In New York City today, the commons may be a pastoral memory of a field, **Central Park**, a paved opening between buildings, Rockefeller Plaza, or a street lined with retail shops and vendors. Our infrastructure is not often thought of in terms of living tissue, but it is nothing less than the vascular system of our cities.

→ SEE MARTENSEN PAGE 26

    The Restorative Commons seeks to apply the restorative qualities of nature to the urban landscape to enhance human and ecological health and well-being. This possibility owes much to the community gardeners who rebuilt the landscapes of our abandoned inner cities in the 1970s and a group of environmental artists who, at about the same time, began creating strong large-scale built works that reminded us of our relationship to the Earth and to nature. While early green infrastructure elements existed in the cellular network of green squares James Oglethorpe designed for Savannah, Georgia, Frederick Law Olmstead's emerald necklace in Boston, and in many other urban parks, these landscapes were not shaped by the culture of cities or to support ecological systems in a concerted way. It was not until we saw large-scale urban gardening through **community gardens** that urban nature began to support neighborhood values, gathering and food production, as well as places for human restoration and healing. The environmental and ecological artists of the 1970s also began exploring large-scale environmental art works that served to highlight natural systems and

→ SEE STONE PAGE 122
→ SEE BENNATON PAGE 232

Curbside gardens
expanded and nurtured
by local residents in
Brooklyn (2006).
PHOTOS USED WITH PERMISSION
BY PHOTOGRAPHER JOHN SEITZ

in some cases worked to restore ecological systems. Savannah's squares and Olmstead's parks were designed primarily for viewing. Nature is to be seen, fixed in approximation of a pastoral ideal, and occupied in equally prescribed measure. The gardeners and the artists changed this paradigm and the elements of a more decentralized, interactive, restorative infrastructure began to appear in our cities.

Earth Art and Community Gardens

In New York City we saw Alan Sonofist's "Time Landscape" completed in 1975 in the West Village and Agnes Degnes "Wheatfield" planted in 1982 in what would become Battery Park City. Both of these large scale environmental works of art introduced another kind of nature into New York City. "Time Landscape" sought to make visible the nature that existed before the settlers arrived and "Wheatfield" created a field of wheat on a pile of rubble on the edge of Lower Manhattan. These projects were instrumental in not only moving art out of the studio and extending the palette to living materials, landscapes, and nature, but also they focused attention on urban ecological issues by integrating the rhythms, seasons, and lifecycles of nature into their designs. As such, these artists refocused us on natural process as a possibility in design. About the same time, a group of East Village gardeners began 'seed-bombing' abandoned lots and organizing the first community gardens. Over the next three decades, as our inner cities were revalued and rebuilt, gardens began to spill over into sidewalk gardens and tree pits.

Tree allee, Brooklyn
Botanic Garden (2001).
PHOTOS USED WITH PERMISSION
BY PHOTOGRAPHER JOHN SEITZ

Streetscape

We also begin to place a higher value on this
"public" nature with neighborhood groups
installing tree guards and competing for
"Greenest Block" honors, a community
outreach program developed by **Brooklyn**   → SEE FIELDS PAGE 231
Botanic Garden's GreenBridge. Trees
began to be valued for an array of ecological
services, as well as their aesthetic value.
These newer valuations included contributions to clean air, ability to support bird
populations, and lowering of summertime
street temperatures.

We are now beginning to see more
attention paid to plantings that can help
clean and manage urban stormwater flows.
In Portland a "Green Streets" program uses
curbside planting areas to both retain and
clean rainwater that falls on streets and
sidewalks.

Rain gardens filter street
runoff in Portland, Oregon.

When these strategies are combined with **building strategies** that may include green roofs, **bio-swales**, rain gardens, and rainwater storage tanks in a comprehensive urban stormwater management plan, we begin to see the potential to significantly alter the urban landscape and restore a productive hydrologic system to everyone's benefit.

→ SEE MARSHALL AND HODA
    PAGE 164

→ SEE LACERTE PAGE 216

Waterways

Sometimes knowledge of an area's natural history will unearth former built-over springs and stream courses. The daylighting of the Woonasquatucket and Moshassuck Rivers, in downtown Providence, RI, included uncovering and restoring two-thirds of a mile of the once covered rivers. In Yonkers, New York State is spending $34 million to daylight part of the Saw Mill River. As we revitalize these water courses, and street and building water flows into the public eye, there are an increasing number of opportunities to not only tell a story of sustainable water management, but also, to begin creatively shaping this infrastructure in resonance with the natural systems and neighborhood cultures they traverse.

Using curbside plantings…green roofs, bio-swales, rain gardens, and rainwater storage tanks…we begin to see the potential to restore a productive hydrologic system to everyone's benefit.

Walls

Public spaces within cities are defined as much
by the walls that border them as they are by
what is within them. Green walls can help us
shape our Restorative Commons from both
an ecological and human health perspective.
Historically most green walls have depended
upon climbing plants that were either able to
cling directly to a wall surface or were aided
by a trellis. This limited the palette to climbing
plants and the height to the reach of the plant.
Recent developments in green roof technology
have extended our ability to support healthy
plantings on walls and we are beginning to
see experimentation in this area; perhaps
most notably by the richly diverse planted wall
gardens of Patrick Blanc.

Ivy on abandoned
building, Newburgh,
New York (2001).
PHOTO USED WITH PERMISSION
BY PHOTOGRAPHER JOHN SEITZ

Greenbelts, Corridors, Greenways

While street trees and our pastoral urban parks have long been valued, it has generally been difficult to integrate an understanding of plant communities and an appreciation for biodiversity into urban planting plans. Three-quarters of the street trees in New York City represent less than 12 species; urban dwellers in both Europe and North America consistently prefer manicured pastoral urban landscapes, and appreciate more diverse alternatives only when they include obvious design elements that indicate human intent. As cities grow and we continue to reduce our biological reserves outside of cities, our urban infrastructures will increasingly be called upon to support plant and animal diversity. In the past some cities created ecological reserves with both leisure and educational components like the Heem parks in Amstelveen, the Netherlands. Today some municipalities are beginning to legislate biodiversity in public plantings and Basel, Switzerland requires that new buildings must not only include green roofs, but must also document diverse rooftop plantings and the ability of plant communities to support specific populations of insects and birds.

Another strategy available to public-space planners is green infrastructure mapping and the coordinated placement of green spaces along corridors to facilitate the movement of bird and animal species. Patch ecology teaches us that the smaller an area of green space and the more disconnected it is from other green spaces, the less it will be able to support plant and animal life. This initial disadvantage can be mitigated by creating green corridors and

Plan of existing
High Line (2002).
MAP USED WITH PERMISSION
OF FRIENDS OF THE HIGH LINE

networks, allowing a mosaic of small green spaces to function more like a continuous edge community. These green infrastructure networks become even more resilient when they are connected to larger natural water or land areas with plant and animal reserves.

As we begin to align open space design and planning with corridor development that includes green infrastructure and pedestrian access, we can begin to understand how the built environment can be shaped to support ribbons of Restorative Commons throughout the city.

Seattle's Open Space Plan for the center city, dubbed the "Blue Ring", is a good example of a U.S. initiative designed to guide development that considers many of these factors and works to put into place a series of linked Restorative Commons. It is successful in large part because it reconsiders the street as open space and prioritizes pedestrians, access to light and air, and an integrated design approach. Designs are to utilize rainwater, consider natural features, be guided by community and neighborhood groups and include public art and healthy green space. In extending these design guidelines to the street and creating an extended ring, Seattle multiplies the potential of these commons greatly.

In New York City, a group of visionaries have created a plan for another green corridor and open space network atop an abandoned elevated railroad. The High Line spans 22 blocks and, when renovations are complete, will create a new raised linear series of gardens and open spaces for a mile and a half through

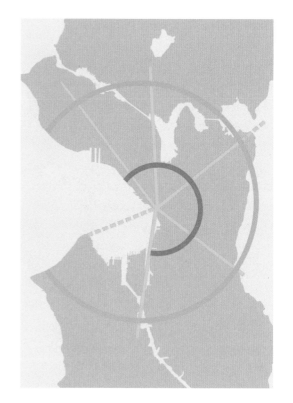

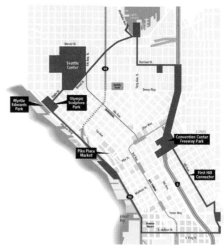

City of Seattle 100-year open space strategy seeks to build connections and create new center city "Blue Ring."

Manhattan. Along the Bronx River to the north, another type of greenway is forming. This one seeks to improve the Bronx River and use the river as a link between a series of new and existing parklands. Plans include improved access to the river, natural area restoration, and conversion of former industrial sites to parkland along the river.

Restorative Commons

The infrastructure of the Restorative Commons is built upon an understanding of natural systems and shaped to celebrate who we are. It is a part of the living world and, like a garden, it requires caretaking, yet it is about more than making sure the plants have sun and water.

We need to find a way to make vibrant and beautiful places in resonance with a nature we once knew: places that engender human health and well-being in both tangible and intangible ways. **Biophilia** helps us → SEE HEERWAGEN PAGE 38 understand our inherent and essential preferences for natural environments, life, and life's processes. These lessons can help shape our commons into places that restore us, that refocus us on the life-support systems that sustain us and that involve, reassure, and fascinate us. These are the environments we need to thrive.

As cities grow and we continue to reduce our biological reserves outside of cities, our urban infrastructures will increasingly be called upon to support plant and animal diversity.

Case Studies

When describing interactions between complex systems
(such as the urban built environment, socio-cultural systems,
globalized economic systems, the biosphere) particularly
at the neighborhood or city scale, it is necessary to draw on
nuanced evidence. Experimental, quasi-experimental, and
quantitative data alone are necessary but not sufficient to
understand the interactions of the urban ecosystem. There
is also a need for textured, qualitative narratives that convey
the *how* behind the relationships that catalyze and the
mechanisms that produce change. To that end, this section
consists of case studies written by practitioners, research
analyzing the practice of others, and first-hand accounts
of project participants.

Creating Restorative Settings: Inclusive Design Considerations

David Kamp, FASLA, LF
Dirtworks, PC Landscape Architecture

The Elizabeth and Nona Evans Restorative Garden
Cleveland Botanical Garden, Cleveland, Ohio

When designers turn their attention to special needs populations, there is a temptation to focus on particular, often restrictive aspects of the project rather than explore the expanse of possible experience. To think of design as providing for all people, it may help to look at health and ill health as a continuum. Some of us have severe restrictions or progressive decline while others have temporary problems or minor, "normal" mobility restrictions. These may range from being in a wheelchair with cerebral palsy to the neuropathy of aging, and from a sprained ankle to maneuvering a baby stroller. When we **design for those with disabilities**, we are, of course, designing for ourselves — or who we may become. In this context, it may be easier to project what we *want* to provide rather than what we *can't* provide.

→ SEE SACKS PAGE 1

Public gardens increasingly seek opportunities to provide more inclusive garden experiences, specifically addressing individuals with special needs. While such opportunities may include programmed activities, such as horticultural therapy, the broader challenge is to accommodate the needs of all visitors in a context that enhances everyone's enjoyment of the garden. One example of a garden that was created to accommodate the full range of the human condition is the Elizabeth and Nona Evans Restorative Garden in the Cleveland Botanical Garden (CBG).

Previous Page:
1100 Bergen Street Garden in Brooklyn shows the site in its neighborhood context.
PHOTO USED WITH PERMISSION BY COUNCIL ON THE ENVIRONMENT OF NEW YORK CITY

Left:
Window portal opening into the contemplative garden invites exploration.
PHOTO USED WITH PERMISSION BY DIRTWORKS, PC

The Elizabeth and Nona Evans Restorative Garden was completed in 2005 on a site created to honor the memory of Nona Evans, a young girl who died in 1958 while she was a student at Sarah Lawrence College. On the death of her mother Elizabeth, the Evans family asked that this lovely, mature "Reading Garden" be redesigned and expanded to provide a garden experience for those with disabilities and that it include space for horticultural therapy.

The Charrette

The first step in this process was a design charrette, hosted by the Cleveland Botanical Garden. It brought together people interested in the garden's design, use, and maintenance, as well as its plant collections, display, and education. Participants included the donor family, key members of the CBG staff including the garden's first-ever horticultural therapist, and a local Cleveland landscape architecture firm that would be involved in the garden's construction. Patricia Owen, who was CBG's current horticultural therapist coordinated the event. Leading the charrette were four landscape designers: Martha Tyson, Vince Healy, Nancy Gerlach-Spriggs, and David Kamp. The charge was to gather and synthesize enough information to develop a design concept for the new garden.

The board of directors, staff, and donors agreed during the design charrette that the garden should be "beautiful, natural, lush, green; a setting that offers a range of opportunities, choices and experiences; a setting engaging and enriching for all who visited." While thoughtfully creating a comfortable environment with a range of uses for all to enjoy, the garden was also to reflect the warm and welcoming spirit of Elizabeth's own garden and terrace.

The charrette set the tone for the project through its collaborative atmosphere and overall vision. During the 2-day work session, important relationships, opportunities, and constraints were identified between the site's unique characteristics, the locations for proposed activities, and the desired ambiance. The resulting concept design addressed these parameters through a strategy of creating three distinct garden settings.

Perhaps most important, the charrette addressed the new garden's context. The garden's 12,000-square-foot area was to fit quietly into the surrounding gardens of CBG as part of a cohesive experience and not as a separate or special encounter. The result is a garden that sits comfortably in its surroundings. As the garden visitor enjoys magnificent views of the surrounding collections, so the surrounding gardens share views of this new, restorative garden.

The charrette also addressed the realities of the site. The space designated for the new garden had 6 feet of grade change and contained a mature plant collection. It incorporated an important view from the library and is located adjacent to what would become a busy dining terrace. Finally, construction would be coordinated with a major building renovation and expansion project under way.

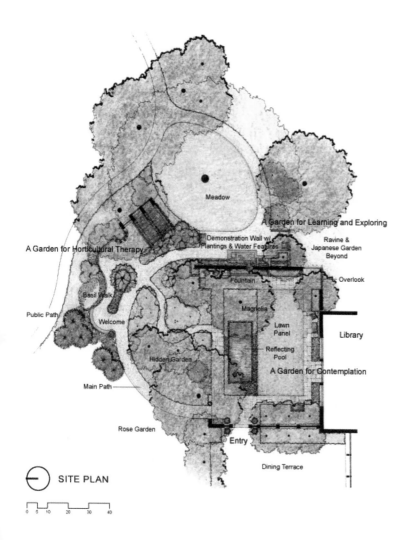

SITE PLAN

The site plan reveals unique gardens for contemplation, learning and exploration, and horticultural therapy.
IMAGE USED WITH PERMISSION BY DIRTWORKS, PC

Design Development and Considerations

Under the direction of David Kamp, the landscape architecture firm Dirtworks, PC designed the garden based on the design strategy developed during the charrette. It responded to several parameters:

- The site's particular opportunities and constraints
- The specific physical and psychological needs of visitors
- The requirements of desired activities and levels of maintenance
- The protection of existing plant material and new plant acquisitions
- The creation of a setting that offers a range of opportunities, choices, and experiences

A close collaborative relationship between the botanical garden staff and the landscape architect were critical to achieving the Restorative Garden's sensitive and responsive design. Dirtworks worked particularly closely with CBG's horticultural therapist and director to identify critical considerations in the design, including program requirements, material selections, safety and privacy issues, and maintenance. This dynamic and productive collaboration was maintained through the project, allowing the designer to consider and incorporate refinements in a timely and cost-effective manner right through construction. For example, grade changes were made to walkways just prior to construction and later on, special stones with interesting textures, colors, and shapes selected by CBG were added to several stone walls.

Design Considerations

Design considerations for the Restorative Garden were based on a simple objective: to provide opportunity and choice for visitors to engage with nature in their own way, on their own terms, and at their own pace. The task was to balance very specific needs with the **simple pleasures of being in nature**. The considerations extend a sense of welcome for every individual, regardless of ability. They offer a sense of familiarity as well as a sense of surprise and delight. The considerations are not intended to look forced or obvious. They are often subtle details, easily overlooked except by those who need them.

→ SEE HEERWAGEN PAGE 38

While some design considerations were specific responses to complement the garden's distinct settings and individual programs, the list below addresses general concerns and patterns that, taken together, help to shape an inclusive garden.

- Consider a range of physical limitations when determining the width of pathways, areas for features or activities, seating types and arrangements, and cues for the vision impaired. Visitors may use motorized vehicles, walkers, or wheelchairs and may have vision impairment, or strength, stamina, or mobility concerns. Throughout the garden, changes in pavement, texture, material, and gradient provide cues to note changes.

- Consider path materials for their durability, aesthetic quality, glare, and accessibility, balancing the need for slip resistance with the degree of texture to minimize fatigue. Path gradients were carefully calibrated to minimize fatigue and provide subtle places to pause and rest and enjoy a fragrance or admire a focal point. Using a paving system that incorporates native crushed stone and pine resin, the pathways provide a unified, natural looking, secure and smooth, low glare surface that connects the garden's various settings.

- Consider what accommodations are necessary to create a sense of welcome and conduct activities without distractions. Depending upon the physical, emotional, and developmental needs of a particular group of visitors participating in a program activity, consider the space needed by caregivers, support people, and volunteers, who might assist participants. Besides specific areas for activities, the garden has several places in which to welcome groups and to talk about a particular feature or activity. These places are generous in size and adjacent to — but outside of — general circulation allowing visitors to pass by (and perhaps listen in) without intruding.

Three Distinct Garden Settings

One of the greatest challenges of this or any fully accessible garden is to provide for all of the just mentioned needs without an overwhelming amount of paving. CBG's Restorative Garden considers all of the above

Design considerations for the Restorative Garden were based on a simple objective: to provide opportunity and choice for visitors to engage with nature in their own way, on their own terms, and at their own pace.

while it remains first and foremost, a garden. It is a place where plants and the supporting elements of water and sky prevail.

The garden is composed of three settings, each with a distinct character and level of activity: one for quiet contemplation, one for individual exploration and teaching large groups, and one for horticultural therapy.

A Garden for Contemplation

The Contemplative Garden serves as the entry point for all three garden settings. Its location adjacent a busy dining terrace requires clear separation. An 8-foot-high vine-covered wall screens the terrace and frames the entry. A "window" in the wall reveals the reflecting pool, magnolia, and lawn, hinting at what is beyond. The space is easy to comprehend and inviting to first-time visitors who discover smaller more private spaces within. This verdant, quiet garden is gracious and welcoming. It is lush; its colors calm and serene. The design reflects the proportion, scale, and fine detailing of the adjacent handsome modern limestone library. The four symbolic "walls" that contain this garden are the floor-to-ceiling windows of the library; an edge of mixed shrubs and two limestone walls; a low retaining wall with a fountain and pool; and the vine covered entry wall. A mature Yulan magnolia (*Magnolia denudata*) stands at the head of a long reflecting pool that sits in a panel of evergreen groundcover. The height of the pool in relation to the adjacent path was carefully considered to allow visitors to see reflections of trees and sky whether sitting or standing. Behind it a fountain flows from the top of the low wall into a basin. The width of the water channel, the distance it falls, and the depth of the basin combine to create a deep, soothing sound that softens nearby conversations. An elegant lawn panel is contained by large sandstone paving stones saved and restored from the original garden. The stone walk connects the entry to seating areas, water features, and an overlook with a view to a deep ravine.

Details were carefully considered to provide seamless accommodation as well as moments of delight. The lawn panel uses a species of grass, supine bluegrass (*Poa supine*), that provides accessibility to individuals in wheelchairs and walkers without the need for in-ground support systems. The horticultural therapist assists

Width, texture, the slope
of paths; height of planting
beds; and views through
the garden are some design
considerations that allow
all visitors to feel safe
and welcome.

visitors to remove their shoes and explore the grass with their toes as they exercise their legs and feet. The path incorporates a raised edge that serves as a subtle guide for those with wheelchairs, walkers, canes and strollers. Large stone paving slabs are laid in a pattern that minimizes joints in the direction and location of wheelchair and walker wheels, thus minimizing the "bump" and fatigue of negotiating joints. An overlook incorporates a custom handrail to accommodate arthritic hands and Braille insets for the visually impaired. The insets feature poems given by friends of CBG and are on the backside of the rails for comfort. The location of the Braille behind the rail adds an element of surprise for those who discover them – both for individuals who read Braille and for those who don't. Outside of the featured magnolia, seasonal color and fragrances in this garden are minimized, creating a relaxing setting with specific but limited sensory stimulation.

Railings with Braille inserts of poetry and garden descriptions.
PHOTO USED WITH PERMISSION BY DIRTWORKS, PC

A Garden for Learning and Exploring

Behind the Contemplative Garden's stone wall is a space with an unusual sense of intimacy. Intended for both individual exploration and group activities, the space is defined by a 6-foot-high stone wall designed in close collaboration with the horticultural therapist and director. It also represents a successful collaboration with the contractor in its detail, craftsmanship, and in the careful placement of interesting stones and planting.

The wall provides privacy and accommodates the grade change between the two gardens and is itself a participatory feature offering many opportunities for touching, smelling, and hearing. Selected native stones, a variety of plants with sensorial interest, and water features — a waterfall, pool, and water trickling over moss-covered stone — engage users whether they sit or stand. The sound of moving water is used strategically here as well. Falling in thin rivulets from the top of the wall into a shallow basin, the water creates a bright, lively sound to screen nearby traffic noise. Plants cascade over the wall and grow in niches. The wall itself steps in height to encourage exercise and develop motor skills while visitors engage in the simple pleasures of smelling and touching as they explore and enjoy this garden. One of the values of the wall and water elements is that it is part of the garden where vision impaired individuals can explore and discover plants independently. The configuration of the wall and water features also creates distinct microclimates providing cues with changes in humidity and temperature.

A Garden for Horticultural Therapy

The space designed for horticultural therapy programs is dynamic. It is sunny, constantly changing, and overflowing with color, scent, and sound, emphasizing sensory stimulation. Therapy clients, some with severe disabilities, work with and enjoy carefully selected plants and activities. Health care professionals and other groups are welcomed in this area to learn about horticultural therapy, plants, and gardening. The general public also has opportunities to participate in programs here.

The organic, curved shapes of the raised plant beds offer generous and easily maneuverable spaces for individuals and groups. Participants have a choice of planter widths, heights, and special displays. Generous

work surfaces provide areas for tools and supplies. The higher raised beds have indented toe spaces so participants can be closer to work areas. Large individual planters enable several participants to work together while allowing easy access for the horticultural therapist, caregivers, and support people. One special feature enjoyed by all is the "Basil Walk". This is a narrow walkway between raised beds containing a dozen varieties of basil that provide a long growing season and dramatic display with cascading plants of various heights and blooms. Visitors, whether walking or sitting in wheelchairs, have the same experience of fragrant basil at eye and nose level.

CBG provides horticultural therapy activities for individuals with cerebral palsy; aging populations with physical challenges or dementia; individuals with vision impairments; adults with severe and multiple physical challenges; autistic youths; and mentally challenged youths and adults. The dynamics of conducting and participating in a therapy activity in such a public setting was carefully considered and is another example of the collaboration between the garden staff and landscape architect. The use of planter walls and planted berms create interest and privacy from nearby paths, allowing the general public to enjoy this garden without distracting groups or activities.

Conclusion

The Elizabeth and Nona Evans Restorative Garden is an integral part of the Cleveland Botanical Garden's mission to blend education, social responsibility, cultural and environmental stewardship helping people of all ages, backgrounds, and abilities appreciate and benefit from the positive role that plants play in their lives. It educates and entertains visitors with sensory rich experiences and programs. It supports and extends the organization's purpose by providing a setting for the collection and display of plants. And most important, the garden does these things discreetly, comfortably, for people of all abilities.

Woman and her guide dog both enjoy the aromas of the planted wall.
PHOTO USED WITH PERMISSION BY DIRTWORKS, PC

The Benefits of Community-Managed Open Space: Community Gardening in New York City

Edie Stone
New York City Department of Parks and Recreation
GreenThumb Program, New York, NY

Community Management is Important

The New York City Department of Parks and Recreation GreenThumb Program (GreenThumb) is the largest community gardening program in the country, serving over 8,000 registered garden members in more than 500 gardens citywide. As the program's director since 2001, I have become convinced that community gardening provides unique benefits to its participants that are distinct from the well documented health benefits provided by traditional parks. These benefits are directly linked with community gardening's ability to provide participants with the opportunities to be actively involved in decision-making about the use and development of the community garden space. As self-governed spaces which are continually changed and modified by their collaborative user groups, community gardens provide many opportunities for exploring novel environments and situations.

Unlike traditional municipal parks and community gardens in some other programs, gardens managed by GreenThumb are true community-managed spaces. New York may go farther than many other cities in its recognition of the rights of community volunteers to set the parameters

Youth in Clinton Community Garden, Hells Kitchen, NY.
PHOTO USED WITH PERMISSION BY PHOTOGRAPHER GLENIS HOLDER, GREENTHUMB

Map of more than 500
community gardens
in New York City.
DATA SOURCE: NYC DEPT OF PARKS
AND RECREATION AND COUNCIL ON
THE ENVIRONMENT OF NEW YORK CITY;
MAP CREATED BY JARLATH O'NEIL-
DUNNE, UNIVERSITY OF VERMONT

Gardeners protesting
on the steps of NYC
City Hall (2000).
PHOTO USED WITH PERMISSION
BY EDIE STONE, GREENTHUMB

of garden management. This is in part a legacy of the political struggle to
preserve the gardens in the late 1990s, when gardeners banded together
citywide to challenge the mayoral administration's plans to develop or
sell the properties. The resulting public outcry culminated in a lawsuit
by the New York State Attorney General, which alleged the gardens' right
to exist as de facto parkland. The settlement of this lawsuit in 2002
included specific language defining the rights of volunteer gardeners
to play an active role in the determination of future plans for the use of
garden spaces. This has led to a general acceptance on the part of the
Parks administration that community garden groups have wide latitude
in determining how their city-owned spaces will be designed, managed,
and used.

The spirit of the New York City community gardening movement
is also very much based in the activist agenda of the late 1970s and
early 1980s when citizen actors decided to take matters into their own
hands to reclaim their decaying neighborhoods. GreenThumb was
established in 1978 as a means for the City to manage and assist the
growing number of gardening groups that had taken over abandoned
city property. From its conception, the program was designed to be
demand-driven, to provide material resources, training, and legitimacy
to citizen volunteer groups who chose to clean up their neighborhoods
themselves rather than wait for municipal intervention (Von Hassel
2002).

Gardeners transformed
dumping grounds and
abandoned lots into
thriving community spaces.
PHOTO USED WITH PERMISSION
BY COUNCIL ON THE ENVIRONMENT
OF NEW YORK CITY

DOME community
garden on West 84th
Street, Manhattan (1979).
PHOTO USED WITH PERMISSION
BY COUNCIL ON THE ENVIRONMENT
OF NEW YORK CITY

The general guidelines for the creation and operation of a GreenThumb community garden are outlined in a license document that is issued by the City of New York to the group of volunteers operating the garden. Beyond these guidelines (which focus primarily on public access and very general standards of maintenance aimed at preventing hazardous conditions), the governance and operation of the gardens is determined solely by the volunteers. As such, the gardens are managed for a variety of uses and functions as recreational, cultural, and educational spaces, as well as places for growing food and flowers.

During the last century, many gardening programs have been started in New York and other cities as part of top-down strategies to assist the poor. These programs, envisioned for numerous purposes including education for schoolchildren, job programs for the unemployed, or war gardens for providing produce during times of shortage, have seldom continued once the crisis they were created to address had passed (Lawson 2005). GreenThumb garden volunteers, however, have shown commitment to continuing to operate gardens over more than 30 years, and to organize politically against the City, when it indicated that the program would be discontinued (Stone 2000). Garden volunteers in New York clearly value their independence and the latitude they are given to govern their own licensed spaces.

Recognizing this independent spirit, I have deliberately taken a hands-off policy regarding the physical and organizational development of individual community gardens. As a civil servant I am committed to ensuring that the gardens, as public lands, provide a public benefit. I am not, however, convinced that anyone other than the garden volunteers themselves can determine which benefit is most needed in their communities. The numerous public programs envisioned, designed, and operated by garden volunteers are implemented with almost no input from GreenThumb staff. Most of the gardens we work with receive less than $600 per year in material support. GreenThumb provides gardeners with access to basic materials necessary to the gardens functioning: access to water, soil, plants, and tools. By employing outreach staff to work with garden groups and organize workshops and events, GreenThumb also provides a human network, someone to call when you have a problem or want to connect with other gardeners.

I believe that this "transforming the dangerous abandoned space into a flourishing garden" story is archetypal; it is a metaphor for the personal transformation many gardeners felt while engaged in the creative process of building and maintaining community gardens.

This is important because the benefits provided by community gardening to the neighborhood — and particularly the benefits provided to the individuals running garden programs — depend, in part, on the gardeners' autonomy from the GreenThumb program. Limiting the material resources we provide creates challenges to the garden group that may ultimately strengthen both group dynamics and individuals' skills. As gardeners strive to find creative, low-cost and culturally appropriate ways to meet the community gardens' operational needs, they gain valuable problem-solving skills and create a network of contacts among garden-supporting individuals, businesses, and institutions in their neighborhoods. Volunteers asked to help maintain traditional parks or gardens operated by groups with paid maintenance staff have no need to develop these skills, and in my experience seldom do.

The success and long-term sustainability of community garden projects depends entirely on the vested interests of neighborhood-based grass-roots volunteers. Disinterest and vandalism are frequent outcomes of urban greening projects implemented without the degree of project buy-in created by giving gardeners broad decision-making latitude in designing and managing their spaces. Equally importantly, the benefits to the gardening individual and community derived from independent and creative decision-making are lacking in projects designed and maintained by neighborhood outsiders, particularly when they are institutional staff or organized, short-term volunteers.[1]

GreenThumb Garden Survey 2003

To document the many benefits provided to local communities by GreenThumb garden volunteer groups, GreenThumb, in partnership with the U.S. Forest Service Northern Research Station, undertook a study of 324 community garden groups registered with the GreenThumb

1. Several gardens built in New York in the 1990s by the Parks Council provide unfortunate examples of this problem. Although the not-for-profit organization attempted to link each garden site with an institution, such as a local school, neighborhood volunteers were not involved in the design or construction of the garden sites. Once the Parks Council staff was no longer present, the garden sites fell into disrepair when local grass roots volunteers showed little interest in using or maintaining them.

Program in 2003 (Svendsen and Stone 2003). GreenThumb staff collected data from garden groups using a standardized assessment. Garden volunteers were asked a series of questions about their use of and feelings about their spaces. The results provided valuable data about how the gardens were being managed and which uses and activities volunteers felt were important to cultivate. When asked what types of events were held in the garden in the last 2 years, groups responded to a list of options, illustrated in the chart (Fig. 2). The types of activities that volunteer GreenThumb gardeners choose to sponsor demonstrate both the needs of the urban communities in which they are located as well as unique and inventive ways to address these needs.

Recreation

It seems obvious that community gardeners would report "recreation" as a top activity taking place in GreenThumb gardens. Community gardening may provide a uniquely beneficial type of recreation, however, because it is unstructured and contains more opportunity for creativity and novel experiences. Unlike traditional parks containing playground equipment or fields designed for organized sports, community gardens encourage creative play and risk-taking in an **unstructured, natural environment**. Leading play researchers believe that risk-taking is an inherent part of play and that we cannot remove all risk from play environments without seriously diminishing their benefit to users. Structured recreation, such as athletics, while beneficial in some regards, does not provide an essential creative element (Brown 1998).

→ SEE HEERWAGEN PAGE 38

Opportunities for rough and tumble play in a natural setting, something that suburban and rural dwellers may take for granted, are often unavailable in urban settings where open space is limited and fear of crime and other dangers cause parents to keep children indoors. A study of convicted murderers illustrated one of the more serious possible outcomes of limiting this type of play behavior — none of the men interviewed had engaged in normal roughhousing as youngsters. The researchers believe that unstructured play helps children understand limits, empathize with others, and determine boundaries (Brown 1998).

By providing safe spaces where children can interact with nature and come into contact with a diverse and multigenerational group of

1100 Bergen Street Garden
in Brooklyn shows the site
in its neighborhood context.
PHOTO USED WITH PERMISSION
BY COUNCIL ON THE ENVIRONMENT
OF NEW YORK CITY

Paradise Garden in the
Bronx shows the use of the
site as a recreation space
and a cultural space.
PHOTO USED WITH PERMISSION
BY ERIKA SVENDSEN, U.S. FOREST
SERVICE

Figure 2

GARDEN EVENTS

Types of events held in community gardens

DATA SOURCE: GREENTHUMB GARDEN SURVEY (2003)

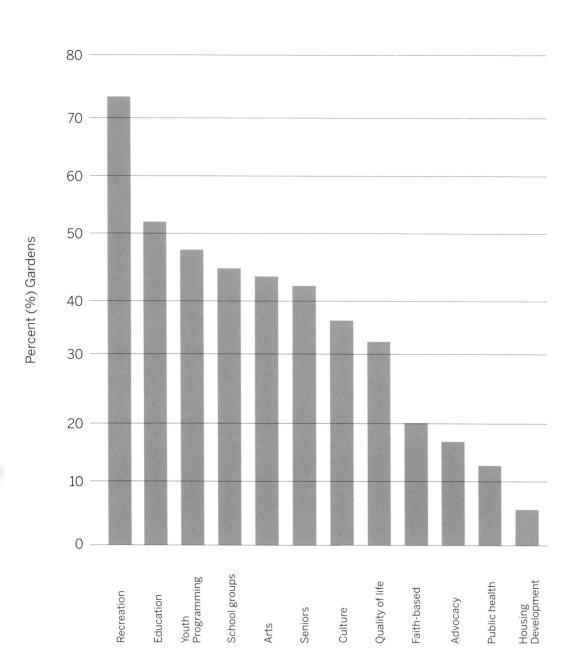

watchful adults, community gardens help provide one of the essential ingredients of a healthy childhood (Louv 2005). Community gardeners I have worked with, regardless of their exposure to academic research on the subject or individual level of education, seem to realize that bringing children into contact with nature is critically important to their development. Many community gardeners have designed their spaces intentionally to meet this recognized need by creating varied habitats for many species. GreenThumb gardens contain fish ponds and butterfly gardens, plantings for bird habitat and forage, as well as quiet seating areas ideal for observing the natural world, and open spaces for kids to run.

Education

For community gardeners, the act of instructing visiting children and adults about the natural world, cultural traditions in agriculture, and gardening techniques also benefits the teacher by providing a sense of expertise and pride. This appears to lead to increased self-esteem and sense of identity for many community gardeners with whom I have worked. The fact that over 50 percent of garden groups reported holding educational activities as well as events for youth and school groups, demonstrates the important role that teaching plays in the lives of community garden volunteers. The fact that GreenThumb does not in any way instruct or require volunteer gardeners to provide educational events also indicates that engaging in teaching and learning is a satisfying pastime for many volunteers.

Seniors

Research on New York City community gardens indicates that many of the volunteers providing these valuable educational lessons to their

→ SEE BENNATON PAGE 232

communities are **senior citizens** (Sokolovsky in press). This is borne out by my own observations. In addition, the 2003 garden survey found that 43 percent of gardening groups reported having events for seniors. Many seniors participate in gardening in New York City as a nostalgic reflection of an agricultural background in childhood as well as to fulfill a desire or economic necessity to grow fresh food. The overall population of community gardeners is also aging. Many New York City community gardens were founded in the early 1980s; as of 2003, 39 percent of gardens were less than 10 years old, 36 percent of gardens were 11-20 years old, and 23 percent of gardens were 21-30 years old. Many, if not most, GreenThumb gardens are still being operated by the original founding volunteers who are now in their 60s and 70s.

Many gardeners in New York City hail from Puerto Rico or the American South where they were actively engaged in farming for their livelihood. Because of events such as the Great Migration, this demographic trend has been observed and documented in other large northeastern cities (Zeiderman 2006). Though their agricultural memories are not always positive, aging gardeners often express an interest in educating their city-raised neighbors about "what it was like." A gardener in Brooklyn who routinely grew cotton in her community garden plot once told me, "I hate cotton—when I left South Carolina I never wanted to see cotton again, but then I thought about all these folks who never had to pick it, and I wanted them to see what we had to do." Nostalgia for a rural past is also reflected in garden names like

Gardener at Hull Street Garden in Brooklyn.
PHOTO USED WITH PERMISSION BY COUNCIL ON THE ENVIRONMENT OF NEW YORK CITY

Figure 3

COMMUNITY ACTIVITIES
Community events in which garden groups participate

DATA SOURCE: GREENTHUMB GARDEN SURVEY (2003)

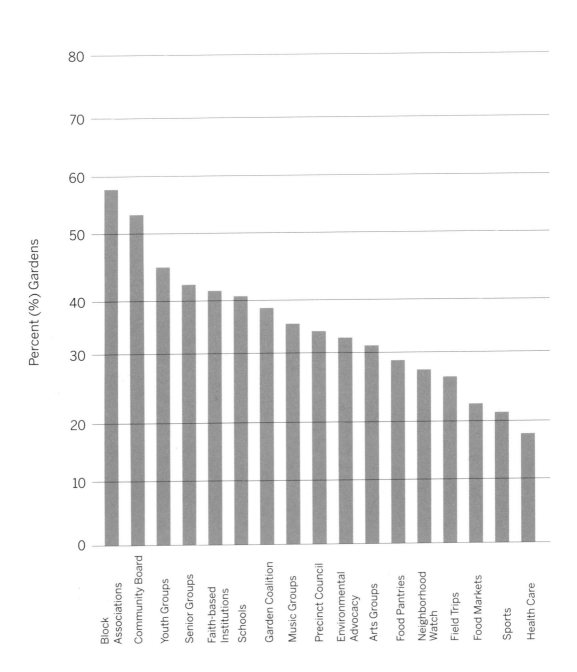

"Down Home Garden," "God's Little Green Acre," and "El Flamboyan," named after a favorite Puerto Rican flowering tree.

In a very real way, seniors who engage in community gardening are remaking a small part of the urban environment into a rural, agrarian society that better reflects their traditional values. Particularly for older adults, research has shown that social integration and the strength of social ties are important predictors of well-being and longevity (Kewon et al. 1998). I believe that participation in the creation and management of community gardens may be particularly beneficial in this regard, as it gives urban seniors a platform to demonstrate their cultural knowledge and history, and to act and be seen as "respected elders" in their communities. The importance of "culture" to community garden groups is illustrated in the 2003 survey results, with over 40 percent of groups reporting holding cultural events.

Health and Social Benefits of Community-Managed Space

Individuals of all ages who are engaged in the creation and implementation of garden programs designed to help others are likely to benefit through the contribution such activities make to their sense of **identity and self-importance**. Many studies have reinforced the important role self-esteem and identity play in promoting health in individuals and communities (Thoits 1991). Participation in altruistic activities, in particular, has been cited as being especially beneficial to individuals by helping to reduce stress, alleviate pain, and improve mental health (Lucs 1998, Dunlin and Hill 2003).

→ SEE MARVY PAGE 202

Volunteer gardeners surveyed in 2003 also reported participation in community-improvement, political, and social activities not related to the garden space. (Fig. 3.) These responses illustrate that gardener volunteers feel empowered to take on additional challenges beyond their garden gates. While the garden survey does not prove causality, I believe it is the experience of having decision-making control over the garden space and the ability to make significant and visible changes there that gives garden volunteers the sense of empowerment they need to participate in leadership activities outside the garden.

By creating a space that has improved their neighborhood in a tangible, concrete way, volunteer gardeners are able to see a beneficial transformation for which they were largely responsible as individuals and groups. The pride garden volunteers feel is evident in the stories they tell. Almost inevitably, a community gardener asked to tell the history of his or her garden begins with the Herculean effort to remove abandoned cars and mountains of rubble and trash. Often emphasizing that "no one helped them, not the police, not the city, no one" garden founders tell of evicting dangerous drug dealers and teaching ill-mannered street children to respect the plants. As community gardens evolved in response to the deplorable conditions in neighborhoods caused by the 1970s fiscal crisis, it is not surprising that **gardeners' stories are similar**. I believe that this "transforming the dangerous abandoned space into a flourishing garden" story is archetypal; it is a metaphor for the personal transformation many gardeners felt while engaged in the creative process of building and maintaining community gardens.

→ SEE SVENDSEN PAGE 58

Lessons for Practitioners

By respecting the experiences, cultural traditions and wisdom of volunteer community gardeners, municipal and nonprofit gardening programs will reap the most benefits for local communities. Organizations like GreenThumb enable and provide legitimacy to the instinctive desire and natural ability of neighborhood residents to improve their physical surroundings by providing a framework for community garden volunteer activity, a physical space to implement it, and minimal material support. GreenThumb provides gardeners with access to the basic materials necessary to the gardens' functioning, and a human support network of outreach workers. By resisting the bureaucratic temptation to over-design community spaces or engage in regulatory micromanagement, support organizations also will increase the mental health and social cohesion benefits community gardening projects provide to individual residents and neighborhoods. Strengthening individuals and empowering local grassroots decision-makers allows community garden support organizations to best contribute to individual health, urban revitalization, and neighborhood cohesion.

Literature Cited

Brown, Stuart. 1998. Play as an organizing principle: Clinical evidence and personal observations. In: Berkoff, Marc; Beyers, John A., eds. Animal play: evolutionary, comparative, and ecological perspectives. Cambridge: Cambridge University Press: 243-259.

Dunlin, P.L.; Hil, R.D. 2003. Relationships between altruistic activity and positive and negative affect among low-income older adult service providers. Aging and Mental Health. 7(4):294-9.

Kewon, B.; Sullivan, W.; Riley, A. 1998. Green common spaces and the social integration of inner city older adults. Environment and Behavior. 30(6): 832-858.

Lawson, Laura. 2005. City bountiful: A century of community gardening in America. San Francisco: University of California Press.

Louv, Richard. 2005. Last child in the woods: saving children from nature-deficit disorder. Chapel Hill, NC: Agonquin Books.

Lucs, Allan. 1988. Helpers high: volunteering makes people feel good, physically and emotionally. Psychology Today. October 1988.

Sokolovsky, Jay. In press. The cultural context of aging, world-wide perspectives, 3rd edition. Westport, CT: Praeger.

Stone, Edie. 2000. Community gardening in New York City becomes a political movement. Presentation at Perspectives of Small-Scale Farming in Urban and Rural Areas-about the Social and Ecological Necessity of Gardens and Informal Agriculture; 2000 July 22; Berlin, Germany.

Svendsen, E; Stone, E. 2003. New York City Parks & Recreation GreenThumb Garden Assessment Report. City of New York Department of Recreation & Parks.

Thoits, Peggy. 1991. On merging identity theory and stress research. Social Psychology Quarterly. 54(2): 101-112.

Von Hassel, M. 2002. The struggle for Eden: community gardens in New York City. Westport, CT: Bergin and Garvey.

Zeiderman, Austin. 2006. Ruralizing the city: The great migration and environmental rehabilitation in Baltimore, Maryland. Identities: Global Studies in Culture and Power. 13: 209-235.

1 mile

Environmental and Community Health: A Reciprocal Relationship

Jeffery Sugarman
New York City Department of City Planning

Fresh Kills Park, Staten Island, NY

The rehabilitation of brownfield sites to productive landscapes — whether for development, pubic open space, or mixed uses — is by its very nature an environmental health undertaking. Contaminant remediation and the creation of cleaner, productive environments on these marginal sites have potential to dramatically enhance the quality of life for some of the neediest, most vulnerable communities. The notion of "Restorative Commons", as articulated by Meristem's Executive Director Anne Wiesen, is one of public landscapes conducive to individual and community health, as well as to lifestyle practices and civic relationships that engage, renew, and sustain such spaces. They are also places and resources to which the public has free and open access. If redeveloped in this way, brownfield projects can strengthen our understanding and respect for the natural environment, heightening our sense of connection to and eventually making us more aware of the interdependence of the human and nonhuman worlds.

Many contributors to the Restorative Commons Forum demonstrated the importance of nature on human well-being and described ways in which this is manifested in people's lives. Ecological and social systems should reflect an active reciprocity between the state of the natural environment and human communities. In brownfield reclamation, I suggest that these benefits come not just from the renewed environment but also from the renewing process itself: there is

Fresh Kills site; an aerial view, looking north.
IMAGE USED WITH PERMISSION
BY CITY OF NEW YORK

a profound and reciprocal relationship between the healing of a natural environment and those enacting it. This is likely on most brownfield projects, but the benefits are most salient where a community is the catalyst for — or has substantive involvement in — the redevelopment. A project such as the making of Fresh Kills Park presents an opportunity to consider how this might happen in complex ways and at a great scale.

From Landfill to Park

Fresh Kills was, until March 2001, the world's largest active municipal waste disposal site, known derisively as "The Dump" by Staten Islanders who, over its four decades of existence, became stigmatized by its presence and revolted by its sight and smell. Eventually, Staten Islanders organized to force the retrofitting of the site with technologically advanced environmental control systems, and finally, the landfill's closure. The former left a "clean" but manufactured landscape of monumental engineering complexity. The impending closure led the City eventually to develop a master plan and conceptual designs for the site's end use after land-filling. At the start of planning it was by no means a certainty that Fresh Kills would become a park, although environmental as well as technical factors made this likely. Its awesome scale and rolling topography, stunning wetlands and creeks, and the sight and sounds of abundant birdlife, made the possibility of a park almost indisputable. Even in its incipient state, the power of resurgent nature expressed in floral recolonization, coupled with a surprising quietude, created a sense of refuge within the city. Further, public testimonial of the sanitation workers over many years, and consultations with policy-makers, designers, and residents during initial reconnaissance visits, revealed longstanding visions of this site as Fresh Kills "Park". Encounter with these was among the most compelling factors in the decision taken to create in this uniquely "urban-pastoral" landscape a public park, despite the challenges, and commensurate with the opportunities of the site's constructed and natural history.

The proposed new park will be almost three times the size of Central Park, comprising four vast waste mounds set within an estuarine landscape of creeks, tidal wetlands, low-lying meadows, and upland forested areas. If successful, Fresh Kills Park promises to be as significant to New York City and the practice of landscape design — and

public health — in the 21st century as **Central Park** was in the 19th and → SEE MARTENSEN PAGE 26
20th centuries. The Park master plan began in 2001 with the selection
of a consultant team, led by James Corner/Field Operations, through
an international design competition that included, even in this early
phase, substantive community input to the design brief. Field Operations'
winning proposal, *lifescape*, envisioned Fresh Kills Park as "a new form of
public ecological landscape; a new paradigm of creativity and adaptive
reuse. *lifescape* was to be informed by the voice of an engaged public
and shaped by time and process." The Field Operations team imagined
an ecologically robust landscape, not as a pastoral refuge from the city,
but as an active agent within it. Fresh Kills would provide richly diverse
settings for wildlife, contribute to urban air quality and efficient water
management, and function as a vibrant locus for social life: for active
recreation and for physical and cultural experiences. Because the site is
vast and complex, the idea of a landscape that would develop in stages,
unfolding over time — as all life does — was central to the competition
proposal and remains at the core of both the draft master plan and early
designs for Fresh Kills Park. Thus, from the very beginning, the Fresh
Kills Park conception embraced design ambitions and strategies that are
clearly, and broadly, health-promoting with exceptional opportunities for
Restorative Commons, for accommodating the functions — social and
biological — that we at the Forum worked to define and understand.

    Judith Heerwagen, another participant in this Forum, described → SEE HEERWAGEN PAGE 38
specific qualities of nature, and our interactions with nature, that
promote a sense of well-being. Some qualities, like those of sunlight and
shade or the proximity of water, are elements in the landscape itself.
Other benefits are generated by our actions in the landscape, a product
of landscape's "transformability" through interactions such as gardening
and plant propagation; the potential for play; or the reordering of the
landscape and elements within it. Many of these attributes are vital to
Fresh Kills Park and its evolution into a refuge not *from* the city, but *within*
the city. Quoting from one of the master plan documents, "This *lifescape*
would be created through human agency — through design and adaptive
engineering, through planning and government investment, and through
the participation of its future users. Sports, learning, performance, and
cultural events, neighborhood revitalization, and art would all take their
place alongside the micro- and macroscopic ecological processes."

Hilltop view, looking north
across William T. Davis
Wildlife Refuge toward
Lower Manhattan.
PHOTO USED WITH PERMISSION
BY CITY OF NEW YORK

...not as a pastoral refuge from the city, but as an active agent within it.

Aerial montage of
the proposed Fresh Kills
Park by the designers,
Field Operations.
IMAGE USED WITH PERMISSION
BY CITY OF NEW YORK

Extensive community input was solicited over 18 months. The plan reflects many of the stated needs and desires of the community:

- Keep the site passive and natural

- Retain the large scale open spaces

- Paths and trails for long walks, cycle rides, and horses

- Access to the water is important

- Limit commercial activities to the core of the site

- Sports and recreation facilities are desirable

- Demonstrate renewable energy

- Demonstrate ecological techniques of land reclamation

The Fresh Kills Park Mission:

- Transform 2,200 acres of landfill to park

- Create a new public park
  of unprecedented size

- Restore the health of 2,200 acres
  of public land

- Establish living laboratory for sustainable
  land practices and infrastructure

- Embody the principles of PlaNYC
  [Mayor Michael Bloomberg's long-term
  sustainability plan for New York City]
  on one site

- Keep a promise to the people
  of Staten Island

The Master Plan

Several goals and strategies of the Fresh Kills Park draft master plan are especially representative of what Restorative Commons should be and warrant close observation over time: the techniques used to revitalize and diversify its wondrous estuarine landscape over many years; revegetation of the landfill mounds to create diverse, native habitats; recreational programming, passive and active, geared to evolving community needs; the degree of, and inventive strategies employed to engage and empower the local and regional community in the site's development; the site's integration into the surrounding natural, human, civic, and infrastructural ecology; and the engineering innovations that will facilitate end use that could have widespread application.

Among the more notable of these efforts, because it will establish the Park's ecological foundation while also presenting remarkable opportunities to make the site's transformation visible, is the mammoth task of soil amendment and manufacture. The draft habitat plan called for a combination of soil strategies: amendment of existing soils, purchase or manufacture of new soils, adjustment of the soil specifications for new cover on the landfill mounds still under-going final closure, even "industrial scale" crop rotation. The latter proposal, successful in Midwest prairie reclamations, turned out to be ill-suited for creation of soils needed by our native plant population; nonetheless it illustrates how keenly the design and planning team understood the fundamental importance of public engagement and how natural processes can uniquely facilitate that engagement: the alternating rows of diverse and colorful crops would have been vividly apparent when seen from adjoining communities and roadways. Quoting again from plan documents:

> "...design as choreography of stages in time... rather than the making of space or place in the traditional sense, is particularly appropriate at Fresh Kills... Especially in a landfill, understanding the stages and processes of transformation is an important public value... The landscape will be 'legible' if the processes of its making are visible, if its appearance carries information about its substance, and if each stage in its transformation is inhabited, understood and enjoyed."

Another example of involving, inhabiting, and reading this changing landscape is the expansion of the city's Native Plant Center at a location adjoining the site and within the adjoining Travis neighborhood. Here many seeds of local origin are being propagated for planting the site, while additional propagation is taking place on site in what is called the "Founder Seed Program." The inclusion of local residents and others from around New York, in this essential act of nature, from seed propagation to sowing of seeds or planting of saplings, also is planned. The use of local seed stock and native plant communities builds on and integrates the site into the surrounding natural ecology.

Fresh Kills Park, in fact, adjoins the existing William T. Davis Wildlife Refuge and will provide the vital, last link in the 3000-acre Staten Island Greenbelt. Given the scale of this effort the project's strategies and outcomes could have global influence on land reclamation, and given its particular location, at the center of the northeastern megalopolis and along the Atlantic migratory flyway, Fresh Kills should provide far-reaching ecological benefits. The plan also calls for — and the Department of Parks and Recreation is now designing into the first projects — sustainable practices for water management, energy production, and energy use. In fact, methane gas at Fresh Kills, a byproduct of landfill refuse decomposition, has long been cleaned and converted to pipeline quality gas for domestzic use. This and other onsite environmental quality control systems will figure in an extensive educational program proposed for the Park.

The central focus on nature and environmental education, passive recreation, and wildlife interpretation at Fresh Kills came directly from the surrounding community and was somewhat surprising given the emphasis on active and competitive sports among Staten Islanders. It was apparent very early in the planning outreach that the local community also felt the unique nature of the site and a need to respond to and learn from it. Fresh Kills Park programming will, nonetheless, be quite diverse, addressing the community's broader needs and taking advantage of the site's particular opportunities. This will include extensive active recreation — such as mountain biking, cultural programming, and public art. The landfill has long had a resident public artist, Mierle Laderman Ukeles, who was on the planning team and championed the need for art and architecture. The Park also will offer

Rendering of proposed
recreational use:
bird observation tower.

Renderings of proposed
recreational uses:
mountain biking, canoeing
and kayaking, soccer fields,
and riding trail.

programming to foster an understanding of waste management as integral to our urban ecology. A park drive, important to site circulation, also was proposed to provide a new east-west link between major arterial roadways, a need long viewed by the community as essential.

Eloise Hirsh, the Fresh Kills Park Administrator for the NYC Department of Parks and Recreation, has said Fresh Kills must be "a model of 21st century infrastructure as well as park development and creation, at the cutting edge of sustainable design; a beautiful park evolving though a very public process." At the same time, she has asked a question that I believe is critical to the making of Restorative Commons, to the building of public parks that optimize community and ecological health: "How do we manage public expectations and inform people of the challenges as well as the opportunities?" I've tried to show through the example of Fresh Kills Park how these opportunities and challenges might be met: for it is integral to the conception, and ultimately, I believe, to the success of Fresh Kills that the human-made environment and natural systems, human and nonhuman habitats, be understood as a single living, experiential continuum. In the words of David Abram, environmental philosopher:

> There is an intimate reciprocity to the senses; as we touch the bark of a tree, we feel the tree touching us; as we lend our ears to the local sounds and ally our nose to the seasonal scents, the terrain gradually tunes us in turn. The senses, that is, are the primary way that the earth has of informing our thoughts and of guiding our actions. Huge centralized programs, global initiatives, and other "top down" solutions will never suffice to restore and protect the health of the earth. For it is only at the scale of our direct, sensory interactions with the land around us that we can appropriately notice and respond to the immediate needs of the living world.
>
> From *The Spell of the Sensuous* (Abram 1997)

The transformation of Fresh Kills will be a literal ground of reciprocity, embodying in its plan and design processes the direct action and interactions of this hopeful vision. In how many ways might we and the environment converse at Fresh Kills and, in so doing, come to a greater understanding of the "encompassing earth" and the impact of our actions within it? At Fresh Kills we have senselessly and severely damaged a previously vital and beautiful ecosystem. But we also have returned, largely through the volition of local communities, to heal that land. This very human impulse to heal seems to me at the core of Restorative Commons, both as a means and end, particularly when the means involve active collaboration of community, policy-makers, planning, and design professionals with, most reassuringly, the land and the air themselves. In so doing we reveal nature's power, our power, to restore health and to take greatest pleasure in our public open spaces.

Literature Cited

Abram, David. 1997. The Spell of the sensuous: perception and language in a more-than-human world. New York: Vintage Books. 352 p.

From Front Yards to Street Corners: Revitalizing Neighborhoods through Community-Based Land Stewardship

Colleen Murphy-Dunning
Urban Resources Initiative, New Haven, CT

New Haven Urban Resources Initiative (URI), a nonprofit organization partner of the Yale School of Forestry and Environmental Studies founded in 1989, works in collaboration with community groups to reclaim our city's environment. Our dual mission is to foster community-based land stewardship, promote environmental education, and advance the practice of urban forestry, as well as provide Yale students with clinical learning opportunities. Our approach through URI's Community Greenspace program combines resident-envisioned urban natural resource rehabilitation, stewardship, and community organizing.

Since 1995, URI'S Community Greenspace program has provided material supplies, technical advice, and classroom-based and hands-on training, delivered by URI staff and Yale graduate student interns, to support inner city New Haven residents who wish to reclaim and then maintain their urban neighborhoods. The interns' learning experiences start months before they ever meet the community. Building upon their course work at Yale, the URI staff augments the interns' knowledge with weekly trainings in local flora, planting techniques, and facilitation skills. In the Greenspace program, URI has paired 97 interns with community groups in the past 13 years. **URI interns** have gone on to work in both the public and nonprofit sector, creating a generation of urban forestry leaders.

→ SEE SVENDSEN PAGE 58
→ SEE JILER PAGE 178

Each year URI works with approximately 50 citizen groups to restore their physical environment, build community, and become stewards of their urban ecosystem. When the program began, URI undertook broad-based community outreach to identify potential stewardship groups, taking out advertisements in local and neighborhood newspapers, conducting mailings to churches and area organizations, and doing presentations at monthly Empowerment Zone meetings. Now that

Greening the streetscape of Cedar Hill, New Haven.
PHOTO USED WITH PERMISSION BY URBAN RESOURCES INITIATIVE

the program has been running for more than a decade, recruitment is less of a challenge and our active outreach efforts have declined. All of the Greenspace sites that URI serves have signage with URI's phone number. We also work through local city Aldermen's offices, performing seasonal outreach. When applications are received, we vet the group to ensure that they are not just single households, but do represent at least an informal group of neighbors, which helps to ensure that groups are committed to site maintenance beyond their own property.

Once groups are identified, community volunteers identify where they wish to work, initiate the greening activity, and undertake all the physical work to implement the planting efforts. Site selection is entirely resident driven and includes historically neglected areas of the city, such as vacant lots, derelict streetscapes, public housing, park land, and even front yards in federally designated Empowerment Zone neighborhoods. The only role that URI plays in site assessment is to ensure that we are serving our priority areas. URI resources are used to support greening efforts on public lands citywide, but are only dedicated to private properties in low income areas.

We support the restoration of this open-ended range of parcels because we are dedicated to community participation in urban ecosystem management, and because all of these parcels make up the urban ecosystem. Furthermore, we are dedicated to broadly engaging citizens across the full spectrum of our populace. Far too often, environmental professionals have set the agenda defining priority areas for restoration and conservation. Doing so has been to the detriment of both the environmental movement, as well as impoverished communities in our society. Creating an opportunity for citizens to define for themselves their environmental priorities is crucial to supporting environmental stewardship as part of citizens' daily life. Yale Forestry and Environmental Studies Professor William R. Burch, the founder of URI, said, "URI takes populations not typically thought of as part of environmental decision-making and shows them that they are."

Reflecting on how participants develop their environmental aesthetic and preferences, I believe it comes from multiple sources. Although community volunteers may not have formal design skills or sensibilities, they universally have a sense of wanting beauty, of wanting a safe place for their kids to play. The housing stock in New Haven is very dense, and often residents do not have substantial private yards on which their children can play, which motivates them to invest in and care for nearby public spaces. Others draw upon their heritage and cultural traditions. For example, many African Americans in the Newhalville neighborhood have extended families in the Carolinas, and some reference the agricultural tradition of the South in their current gardening works. Other residents are immigrants who bring the traditions of their places of origin to their current greening efforts, such as Puerto Ricans in New Haven who select certain colors and plants that remind them of the island. To expand our participants' understanding of what is possible on their sites, we set up tours of other Greenspace sites. In this way, volunteers learn from each other as peers, share information, get ideas, and engage in social networking. We have also taken Greenspace participants to visit local parks, and have used print media — like gardening magazines — just to offer inspiration and starting points for dialogue.

New Haven is home to six Enterprise Zone communities, a federal designation of poverty. Just as there is an economic disparity between these low-income neighborhoods and wealthier neighborhoods, there are also stark differences in educational attainment. Low-income urban communities, in particular, face many challenges and are often characterized by drug dealing, high rates of incarceration, high school truancy and high drop-out rates, type 2 diabetes, asthma, unemployment, and prostitution. These same communities are often physically described by blight, graffiti, and derelict structures. While a causal relationship between many physical and social attributes are difficult to establish, anecdotal evidence exists on improving human health and well-being by improving the physical condition of neighborhoods.

The small New Haven neighborhood known as Cedar Hill by those who live there is not well known by those who don't. In 1960, the construction of Interstate 91 suddenly isolated the community. In 2004, a small group of neighbors from the Cedar Hill blockwatch mobilized to plant street trees. Illicit activities occur at some of the nearby business establishments, and prostitution occurs in cars parked in Cedar Hill that come off of State Street. Despite these challenges, the group takes great pride in both their work and in their neighborhood. While they

Creating an opportunity for citizens to define their environmental priorities is crucial to supporting environmental stewardship as part of citizens' daily life.

are very serious about combating the illegal activities that diminish the quality of life in their neighborhood, they carry out their planting work in a playful way. Perhaps it is the laughter and joy that is always present when they work together that seems to heal the social ills as well as the personal health struggles some of their members' face. There is a growing body of evidence that the experience of being in nature, even urban 'nearby nature', is healing on many levels. Feelings of safety and interconnectedness allow the flow of laugher and personal joy that so often spontaneously occur when working on nature projects. Sociologist Eric Klinenberg's (2003) research on the 1995 Chicago heat wave found that the most socially isolated individuals — particularly shuts-ins and seniors — had the highest morbidity and mortality rates. These processes that were magnified and made clear through an extreme weather event may indeed be at work on a day-to-day basis. Klinenberg discovered what we know intuitively to be true in neighborhoods where URI works: social bonds, social capital, and social cohesion affect individual and community health.

Or, perhaps it is the tangible, visible changes they have accomplished that are at the root of their healing. Their accomplishments include creating a median planting as the gateway from the park into their neighborhood; planting street trees where prostitutes formerly worked; and planting a garden area at a former dumping ground near the highway (they refer to this area as 219 — because there is a sign posting a $219 fine for dumping at the site). Compost piles are strategically placed where previously cars parked to allow for quick sex acts to be carried out. Likely these physical transformations have helped the neighbors feel better about their community. This is clear to any visitor to their website, which one of their blockwatch members developed. Indeed, it is hard to miss the "I Love Cedar Hill" mugs and t-shirts for sale in local businesses.

In general, many groups talk about how much better they feel about their communities because they are able to make positive change — even if it is only aesthetic. They say that they feel more in control — a word that can be taken in many contexts. First, it is important to recognize that many stewards do engage in community greening work out of basic concern for the safety and security of themselves, their family, and their property. A large proportion of the

Greening the streetscape
of Cedar Hill, New Haven.
PHOTOS USED WITH PERMISSION
BY URBAN RESOURCES INITIATIVE

neighborhood groups with which we work are blockwatch groups, which are essentially community networks that were created to control crime. These block groups see controlling the visual landscape as one more effort to reduce crime. Secondly, and perhaps more universally applicable to the question of health, we are talking about the need to have control in the social environment, using the physical environment as a means to gain that control. I have observed that when people feel victims of their surroundings, or their medical diagnosis, they may feel they have lost some control over their life. Moreover, broad social and environmental trends, such as the economic downturn and the energy crisis, will affect these places the most, causing more people to live in situations without control, essentially as 'victims of their environment.' Even if neighborhood greening is only a symbolic gesture, they feel better because they can see they have affected change. As Burch has said, "One of URI's major outputs is human dignity and empowerment."

In the summer of 2007, I conducted an interview with two members of the Cedar Hill Blockwatch Association to discuss why there were involved in the Community Greenspace program and what impact it had on their lives. Both women are senior citizens, African American, and both are cancer survivors. It is clear that they find comfort in the physical labor of gardening as well in the social interactions of working to improve their own neighborhood. Despite both women having lifting restrictions placed on them by their doctors due to their cancerous lymph nodes, they engage in vigorous planting activities weekly. Throughout the phase of diagnoses, treatments, and recovery, these women looked after each other and their neighborhood streets in reciprocal acts of caring.

Sue[2] is a lifelong gardener and community volunteer who has been involved with a variety of church and school groups. Her environmental stewardship work is embedded in and linked to other acts of community organizing and civic engagement; she regularly attends city hall meetings to advocate for a number of neighborhood concerns. She became aware of the URI program through her work pushing the city to install new sidewalks in the neighborhood. Since URI's Community Greenspace application requires a minimum of four neighbors as

---

2. Name has been changed.

sponsors, Sue engaged her neighbor, Karen, in the group.

Karen[2] said that Fridays, planting days, always brighten up her week. Planting keeps her going, happy, and inspired, at a time when her illness could do just the opposite. She felt that seeing the look of surprise and appreciation on her neighbors' faces had a positive impact on her health. She said "gardening, to me, is wellness." Karen wrote the following narrative — with the help of her daughter — about her experience in battling cancer. She believes that gardening, battling cancer, and life in general are all acts that require strength and faith:

> "I was asked to remember about a period in my life when I was in a full-fledged battle against an invasion inside my body. A body that I worked hard to keep safe from certain attacks (or so I thought). I never smoked, drank or practiced certain behaviors that society has taught us may harm this precious temple we call the body. But, it was always hidden way, way back in that place in our minds where we place the scary items. The fears, the things we never hope to face and definitely not have to fight. Then, I embraced a walk with two old friends I had known all my life, Grace and Faith. Grace to get through and Faith to believe I would. And then healing began. I walked out on Faith, led by Grace. I'm still here, and it must show. God picked me out of his garden, tore away the weeds and started afresh. It began with my own gardens. At first it was hard to discern what weeds were, what needed to be plucked away, what could be saved?
>
> And just as gardens grow, others in my neighborhood with like minds joined together and we have started to beautify with great stewardship, areas that were neglected. My favorite quote is 'gardeners are people who believe in tomorrow.'"

Karen is helping to bring that future-oriented outlook to the development of the URI program, by serving on the board of directors. Her input and insights will grow the Community Greenspace program for many other neighborhoods and groups like her own.

Future/Frontier

The complex and multifaceted relationship between individual health (both physical and mental), community cohesion, and urban design is still being explored — both in academia and in field projects like ours.

However, even in the case of environmental health issues with known causal relationships, the implementation of new programs to address those issues is far from finished. For example, URI recently tested soils for contaminants at 50 community project sites. We found 90 percent of sites have both lead and arsenic present beyond acceptable federal standards (for lead, the Environmental Protection Agency [EPA] standards are 400 ppm for play areas, and 1200 ppm yard wide). Contaminated soil is commonly found in barren urban locations and easily transforms into dust, which can be tracked into houses or suspended in the air. The dust can be inhaled or ingested by hand-to-mouth contact, contributing to heavy metal and/or pesticide poisonings, asthma, and even diseases such as ringworm, roundworm, and *E. coli* from pet fecal matter in the soil. There is a known relationship between lead exposure and negative affects on human brain development, particularly among children.

New Haven has the highest number of reported cases of children with elevated blood lead levels in Connecticut, which is due to both the age of the housing stock in the community combined with the prevalence of poverty. The city has over 400 current cases of lead poisoning 10 micrograms per deciliter or higher. New Haven's Health Department tracks these children, documenting their blood lead levels by census tract and age. Unsurprisingly, the census tracts with highest numbers of cases of children with lead poisoning coincide with the neighborhoods where URI actively partners with community groups to recover their degraded landscape. Currently we are conducting outreach to renters and homeowners to raise awareness of the problems associated with polluted soils, sampling and testing soil in 50 front yards, and conducting remediation where needed. Following this testing program, we developed an effort to remediate sites and educate residents about exposure reduction techniques. We've nearly completed the remediation phase, and have learned alongside the neighbors how difficult this task is.

There are limitations, however, as to what can be accomplished through actions led by URI and our community partners. Operating in a city of scarce resources, our program does not have the capacity to test, let alone remediate, all of the yards and play spaces in New Haven that are exceeding federal standards for lead. While we intend

to raise awareness, provide testing, and develop broadly applicable
field protocols for remediation, there is a need for public resources to
address these environmental conditions at a larger scale. Contamination
on private, currently occupied residential lands may be the next frontier
in the already complicated realm of brownfield sites, Superfund sites,
and other toxic sites.

*   *   *

The Oscar-winning film "An Inconvenient Truth" was a brilliant tool
to increase the public's *understanding* of global warming. Yet, changing
behaviors and *lifestyles* is a more difficult step that must be taken.
The now-old adage of "think globally, act locally" continues to resonate.
Again, environmental professionals will not solve such ecological crises
with only policy tools. Finding ways to engage individuals to be stewards
of their community — or "building a cadre of nature stewards" in
the words of William Burch — is our means. If we can connect people
to their landscape, and support their healthy relationship to the land,
we can hope to solve both global concerns as well as support the
human community.

Creative Uncertainty

Victoria Marshall
TILL Design

Dil Hoda
Monroe Center for the Arts

Monroe Center for the Arts, Hoboken, NJ

Monroe Center for the Arts is a mixed-use, market-driven real estate development project in Hoboken, New Jersey. It offers an urban design model for neighborhood change that actively cultivates ecosystem stewards through design with water and a measure of success called creative uncertainty. Water, which is not currently a positive presence in the neighborhood, is repositioned as an attractor. The meaning of this new water is intentionally immediate, multiple, ephemeral, and ambiguous.

Creative uncertainty as introduced by Felix Guattari is a mode of activism that aims to engage "How interrelations between living systems, social structures, and psychical processes are conceived" (Gensko 2003). This is not a goal toward fixity and control but rather toward the production of difference and heterogeneity. What is foregrounded at Monroe Center for the Arts therefore is not conservation of environment, but rather conservation of the view that environment is a living and changing system continually influenced by living and changing ideas. This is our commons and we wish for it to be continuously produced and recreated.

A 5-acre development, Monroe Center for the Arts currently hosts 70 artists and 50 businesses. Starting in 2008 the population density and level of use will increase by the addition of three new buildings, a public space with two fountains, and roof gardens. To communicate the design intent of Monroe Center, this text introduces the project as fully built, although it is still currently in construction.

An overlay of the former coastline reveals that Hoboken was once an island in the Hudson River.
IMAGE USED WITH PERMISSION BY VICTORIA MARSHALL, TILL DESIGN

The structure of this essay mimics the pathway of rainwater through the project; by describing water-human networkings in everyday scenarios starting from far above the ground, to on-the-ground surface, and finally into the ground's subsurface. In addition the legal, financial, and environmental mechanisms of this project are shared to make legible the way in which this hydrology design process was started by the developers 14 years ago, has been taken up by the landscape architect, and will be handed over to the new residents. The intent of this essay is to communicate our belief that new natural resources can be produced by humans. The traditional understanding of a natural resource is therefore being expanded to include human and societal mechanisms for caretaking.

Design: Tilling

Water in the west edge of Hoboken is the substance that lingers in the street after a storm. Close observation reveals that this water is

sometimes a rainwater pond and other times a brackish pool. This is because the composition of the water depends on the confluence of a local rain event and the Atlantic Ocean-Hudson River high tide. In these coincidental events, water forms a discontinuous surface, temporarily marking the ancient wetland river edge. It is an enigmatic urban actor and it is the inspiration for a flexible and adaptive public space network at Monroe Center for the Arts.

The existing and new neighborhood artists, residents, and users act in multiple ways to generate and share knowledge about their watershed. In a crisis scenario, excess water is considered a liability, such as a harmful flood. Conversely, in the context of this new development, excess water creates new opportunities for recreation, relaxation and exchange. People here appropriate their various public surfaces in innovative and playful ways.

Starting from the highest elevation, the new residents in the condominium towers are the high-rise caretakers of the watershed.

Looking toward the Palisades, the Hudson River estuary high tide is periodically visible in the Monroe Center parking lot.
IMAGE USED WITH PERMISSION BY VICTORIA MARSHALL, TILL DESIGN

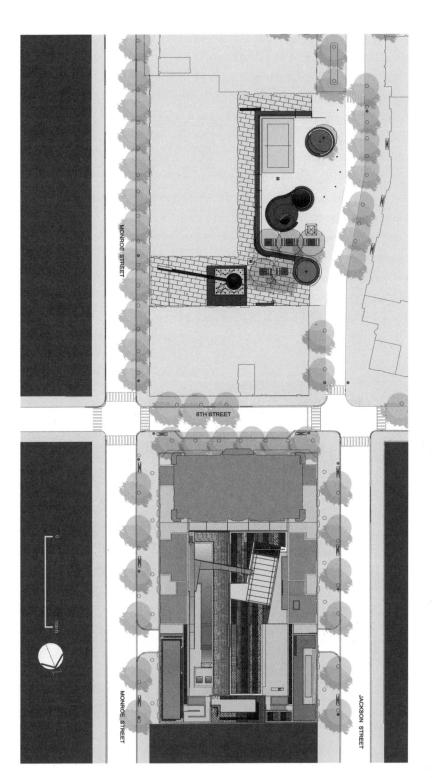

The Monroe Center
site plan shows the
transformation of
a former factory to a
mixed-use, vegetated and
inhabited development.
The productive nature
of the industrial land
is updated with design,
small businesses,
and arts practices.
IMAGE USED WITH PERMISSION
BY VICTORIA MARSHALL, TILL DESIGN

They protect the headwaters of the condominium tower catchment with their balcony rainwater filtration gardens and management of patio surfaces with nontoxic cleaning products. This water is stored in a basement tank and is used to irrigate the roof garden. In addition, balcony gardens provide extended habitats for birds and bugs migrating across the street from the Palisades cliff. Given their broad horizon, the high-rise tenants also serve as benefic surveyors, monitoring the neighborhood roof garden terrain.

The Palisades cliff, an ancient geologic fault, marks the boundary between Hoboken and Jersey City. Extending from Jersey City to far upstream on the Hudson River, the Palisades is a linear forest inhabited by plants, animals, and people. Due to its topography, it is difficult to navigate, however a carefully constructed trail has begun, which will eventually offer an urban hike to Bear Mountain, 50 miles north. Physically traversing this slope provides a performed measure of the river and its watershed. The trailhead is located at Monroe Center and is being created by an overlapping network of stewardship organizations.

The next watershed caretakers are the high-rise rooftop garden users. Encouraged to appropriate the roof as their own yard, they continuously invent practices and adapt their lifestyle on top of its thin absorptive section and in its gentle microclimate. Paved, grassy, sand, and gravel surfaces afford typical programs such as reading, walking, or play, however, as an extension of the Monroe Center for the Arts the same surface can function as a yoga studio, art class, ballroom, gallery, or whatever the creative users imagine. Two mobile barbeque carts and a cabana provide a cooking and washing surface for a roof top brunch, wedding, or even a mini-restaurant.

Accessed from the fifth floor via a public elevator and the fourth floor via the resident corridors, the roof garden has three distinct levels. The fourth floor terraces are like outdoor rooms, one with grass and the second with sand and toy boxes for play. Ramps and a stair allow access to the four-and-a-half floor wet garden and the fifth floor dry garden. Like an elongated zigzag, the circulation system is designed for both evening neighborhood strolls as well as a place to be still.

The roof garden functions to mitigate ground-level flooding as well as to offer a higher ground refuge during surge events. Located over a parking garage and residential apartments, it is on average 1-foot

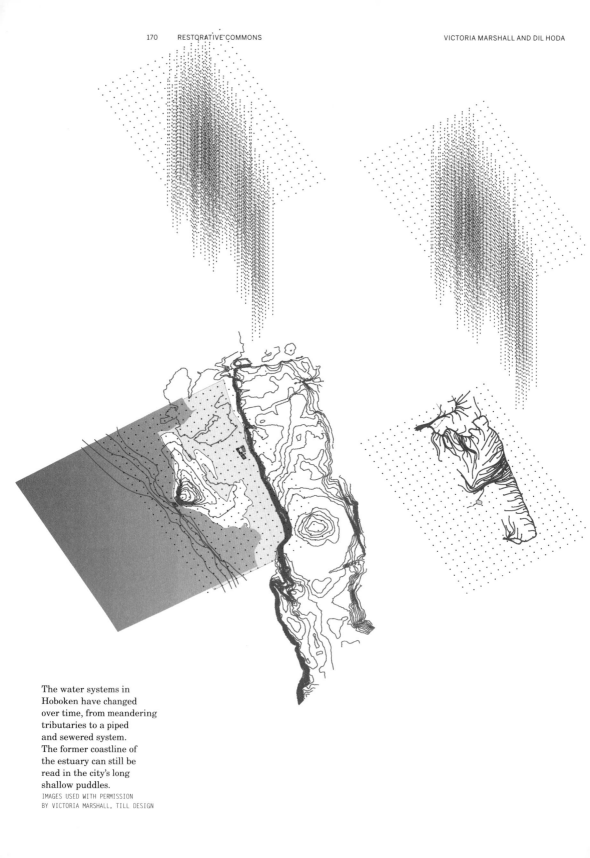

The water systems in
Hoboken have changed
over time, from meandering
tributaries to a piped
and sewered system.
The former coastline of
the estuary can still be
read in the city's long
shallow puddles.

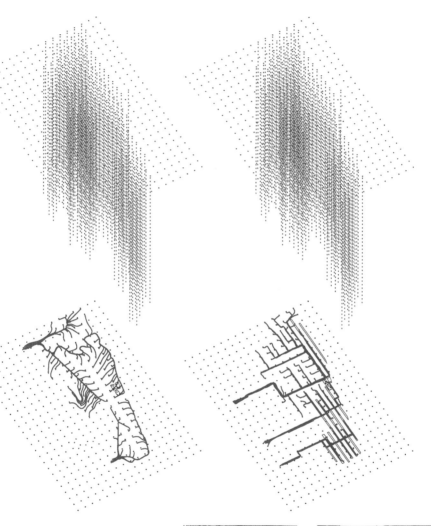

thick with multiple waterproofing membranes. An extensive green roof system acts as a sponge absorbing water and releasing it slowly. Hot water, created via a heat exchange with the warmer temperature in the earth is released into a fountain. This geothermal fountain also functions as an informal bathing pool. Adjacent are two hot tubs and a shower nook. Hot and cool water are therefore used to entice extended fall and spring season use, and a mobile fire pit is available for year-round use.

The street level stewards are the commuters, shoppers, tenants, restaurant patrons, retail owners, and workers. The rhythm of joining the breakfast crowd, lunchtime crowd, dinner crowd or the after-hours crowd affords opportunities for long-term, everyday, peripheral watershed observation. Two plaza fountains hold and circulate stored rainwater. Like large clocks, they evaporate slowly, measuring the moisture changes through subtle shifts in the splash of a mini-waterfall and the bubbles in a pool. The plaza consists of two levels; the boundary between them is the ancient Hoboken Island shoreline. Like an amphitheatre, the upper level is designed to offer a place to observe people and natural processes on the lower level. When the tide comes in, the water becomes the performer, filling the lower plaza. In another scenario, stored rainwater used for irrigation allows the plaza vegetation to sustain periods of drought. The Monroe Center for the Arts, therefore, manages heat and water stress that would otherwise negatively affect vulnerable populations, such as the elderly, and natural resources, such as street trees and gardens.

Below the plaza level, under the built-up and sealed surfaces and into the groundwater, there is another natural process occurring and being followed by the residents. Monitoring wells on top of the clay layer at 20 feet below grade and at bedrock (around 100 feet below grade) are regularly checked for the presence and absence of water and contaminants. Given the industrial legacy of the area, there is a slowly migrating flow of contaminants across property boundaries. On a regular basis, environmental consultants sample the wells and report their findings to the residents and public agencies. This aquatic uncertainty is therefore made transparent and allows for precaution and feedback.

An example of ecosystem feedback has already occurred. During the construction of one of the residential towers, elevated levels of trichloroethylene (TCE) were detected in the subsurface water. TCE, a degreaser component, is unhealthy for human contact. After multiple attempts to neutralize the TCE and its derivative products, a cut-off wall was built below one of the buildings. Most of the water that was perched on top of the impervious clay layer within the cut-off wall was pumped out.

Development: Method

The Monroe Center for the Arts site was formerly the Levelor Blinds factory. With its two mill buildings and the surrounding 4 acres of land, it was blighted and slated by the local municipality for eventual demolition and construction of luxury housing. The owners of the site, with the support of the existing artist community in the buildings, proposed a mixed-use development that would be anchored by artists and the arts. This entailed preserving the arts community and constructing affordable work/ live spaces for artists, as well as taking the arts out into a public plaza and roof garden.

Environmental remediation was funded primarily through a combination of the Brownfield Reimbursement Program (BRP) and the New Jersey Environmental Infrastructure Trust Financing Program (EIT). The BRP (a state of New Jersey program) permits the reimbursement of 75 percent of the sales taxes generated on the site for 75 percent of the remediation costs. The EIT is largely funded by the EPA's Clean Water State Revolving Fund, which provides "seed money" for the state agency. New Jersey has used these funds to provide low-interest loans for 20 years. Until recently, the EIT funds were used primarily for municipal utility projects; since 2004 the program has been expanded to include brownfields and non-municipal water-cleansing projects.

To compensate for the development of the affordable units and the public space, the owners requested and received Payment in Lieu of Taxes (PILOT). Under the PILOT, the property tax burden (consisting of municipal, county, and school taxes) is reduced by eliminating the school tax and substantially reducing the county tax. Overall this new development generated substantially higher tax revenues for the city in absolute numbers. The public space and the rooftop gardens, in turn, created the opportunity for the fountains, the design of which would cleanse the water and therefore qualified for funding under the EIT.

Two plaza fountains hold and circulate stored rainwater. Like large clocks, they evaporate slowly, measuring the moisture changes through subtle shifts in the splash of a mini-waterfall and the bubbles in a pool.

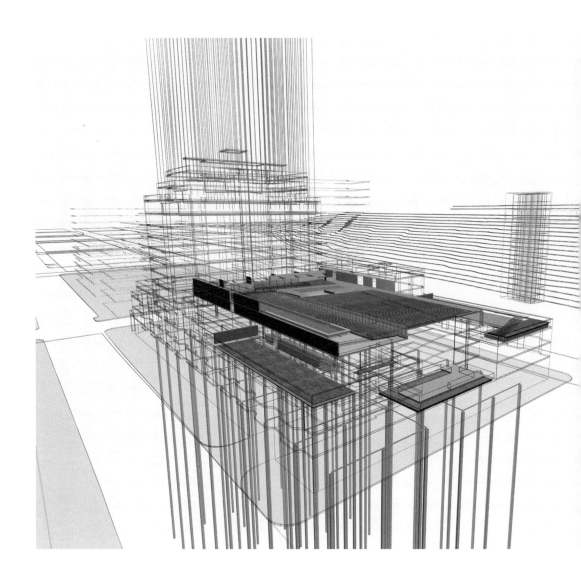

The Monroe Center roof
garden harvests rainwater
(blue), municipal water
(pink) and geothermal
heat and cool (orange.)

The fountains and the arts, both in the public plaza and roof gardens and within the buildings, are attractive to the retailers and the market-rate home buyers and renters. The retailers started generating the sales taxes for reimbursement under the BRP. The market-rate housing generated the property taxes for the PILOT, which can be used for an up-front bond issuance for infrastructure as well as payment of the EIT loan. Thanks to municipal, state, and federal funding programs, support of the local neighborhood, and nesting of the various funding programs and programming of the overall development, local artists, market rate homeowners and renters, over 2,000 residents of a nearby public housing complex and visitors enjoy water and its myriad manifestations.

Conclusion

This project is designed with an understanding of health that is informed by contemporary ecosystem science where urban ecosystems are viewed in a non-equilibrium paradigm (Walker and Salt 2006). That is, they are **resilient**, complex, socio-natural, adaptive systems rather → SEE SVENDESEN PAGE 58 than one self-regulating system. In contrast to a conservation strategy of protecting remnant or restoring degraded water or plant systems, this is a mode of working that is more projective toward yet-to-be imagined futures and inclusive of social and economic forces. We ask of our work, can healthy urban ecosystems be designed with monitoring, knowledge, and feedback, as well as continuous planning, invention, adaptation, and wonder? The role of design is therefore shared and does not lie in the hands of one professional at one point in time. However we do believe that a compelling urban design made at one moment in time can function as a long-term ecosystem management tool by actors in everyday life.

Water is a material that triggers creative uncertainty and therefore it offers the critical ecosystem process of multiplicity. By this we mean:

"[N]ot the H_2O produced by burning gases nor the liquid that is metered and distributed by the authorities. The water we seek is the fluid that drenches the inner and outer spaces of the imagination. More tangible than space, it is even more elusive for two reasons: first, because this water has a nearly unlimited ability to carry metaphors and second, because water, even more subtly than space, always possesses two sides... water remains a chaos until a creative story interprets its seeming equivocation as being the quivering ambiguity of life. Most myths of creation have as one of their main tasks the conjuring of water. This conjuring always seems to be a division"

Illich 1985

Ecologists Steward Pickett and Mary Cadenasso (2007) write about the role of meaning, model, and metaphor to communicate science concepts to "the public, to specialists in other disciplines, and even to schools of ecology beyond those which generally use it." At Monroe Center, our notion of the commons references this three-part thinking: the meaning we seek is to design public spaces that keep open the 'window' of creative uncertainty for the users; circuits and feedback loops of everyday life offer an urban design model for adaptive ecosystem management; and finally, water is the material that brings forth competing and collective metaphors toward building communication, trust, and cooperation.

In the future it is planned that this multi-dimensional model of development will be translated to other sites. While every landscape has water, this does not necessarily mean that it should always be the organizing element. Other attractors could include, for example, nitrogen or carbon. While not as charismatic as water, the role of design in these landscapes would need to work harder, requiring more fantastic and spontaneous scenarios of our possible urban lives. In addition, the integration of science models into design—and therefore seeing designs as working models of a small part of an urban ecological system—offers approaches to complex ecosystem processes in spatially based and meaningful ways.

Literature Cited

Gensko, G. 2003. Felix Guattari—toward a transdiscsiplinary metamethodology. Angelaki, Journal of the Theoretical Humanities. 8(1): 129-140.

Illich, I. 1985. H_2O and the waters of forgetfulness—reflections on the historicity of stuff. Dallas: Dallas Institute of Humanities and Culture.

Pickett, S.T.A; Cadenasso, M.L. 2007. Meaning, model, and metaphor of patch dynamics. In: McGrath, B.; Marshall, V.; Cadenasso, M.L.; Grove, J.M.; Pickett, S.T.A.; Plunz, R.; Towers, J., eds. Designing patch dynamics. New York, NY: Columbia University Press: 24-25.

Walker, B.; Salt, D. 2006. Resilience thinking—sustaining ecosystems and people in a changing world. Washington, DC: Island Press.

We ask of our work, can healthy urban ecosystems be designed with monitoring, knowledge, and feedback, as well as continuous planning, invention, adaptation, and wonder?

Restoring Lives, Transforming Landscapes: The GreenHouse Program at Rikers Island Jail

James Jiler
Horticultural Society of New York

Rikers Island, New York, NY

Kamelita M. stood by a planter box of yellow mums, boxwood, and ivy on a residential street in Greenwich Village. In a dark blue shirt, khaki pants, and carrying a black canvas gardening bag, Kamelita snipped ivy and pruned out errant branches in a meticulous manner. It was a striking fall day, warm with a cloudless blue sky. As a plant technician for a private landscape firm, Kamelita would earn $17 an hour for her work. Ten blocks north, Manual R. planted several hundred bulbs in one of New York City's premier public spaces, the newly restored Madison Square Park. Employed by the Madison Square Park Conservancy, Manual was an integral part of a process to build high quality gardens in public parks through public/private partnerships across the city. What makes these individuals notable, however, is not so much the work they were doing, but the path they took to arrive at work; for only 1 year before, both Kamelita and Manual were inmates at The New York City jail complex on Rikers Island, serving a year for stolen goods and drug possession.

During their incarceration, Kamelita and Manual joined the GreenHouse Program, a jail-to-street horticulture project run and administered by the Horticultural Society of New York (HSNY). Unlike most prison farms, often evocative of men toiling in endless rows of leafy crops with guards on horseback, GreenHouse operates

Rikers Island garden, circa 1998 (*top*) and 2007 (*bottom*).
PHOTO USED WITH PERMISSION BY JAMES JILER, HSNY

under a different premise. Here, at a 2-acre facility and greenhouse on Rikers Island, men and women inmates learn the art and science of horticulture. The programmatic approach provides education, vocational skills, and ongoing garden therapy as a way to help inmates redirect their lives in a positive and productive manner. The physical result is nothing less than remarkable: in 10 years, a weedy, barren lawn has been transformed by 550 inmates into bird and butterfly gardens, a native forest, herb and vegetable gardens, a peace pagoda

→ SEE CAMPBELL PAGE 188

for **Sept. 11, 2001**, a pond, waterfall and gazebo complex, all traversed and tied together by a series of elegant pathways. The concept of "transformation" is inherent in everything that takes place in the garden, for in the process of transforming landscapes, the students begin the process of transforming themselves.

Equally important is the objective to change the concept of jail, which — in the parlance of ecologists — is seen typically as a resource sink, or as one correction official liked to comment — "a graveyard of lost opportunity." GreenHouse operates under the premise that jail can serve as a sustainable resource — one that generates benefits to constituents in jail as well as to entire communities across the city and region.

Doing their "time" in the garden, inmates will not only rehabilitate themselves but rehabilitate damaged plants given to HSNY by nurseries or landscapers all over the New York region; grow plants (annuals, perennials, herbs and vegetables) for community groups in New York City; from salvaged wood, construct nesting boxes and bat houses for city parks and open space to improve habitat for native wildlife; build rooftop gardens in jail that will later be reassembled for city schools or community groups; and after their release, bring their gardening skills back to their families and neighborhoods.

By connecting people who have had little contact or understanding of nature to the natural world, the GreenHouse Program hopes to combat the 65 percent recidivism rate that has plagued the country's criminal justice system (Elsner 2004). And while the connection is profound, the hard skills of horticulture need to be employed when the inmate leaves jail and is faced with the myriad of poor choices available in inner-city neighborhoods. It is well documented, for

An inmate maintains the garden.
PHOTO USED WITH PERMISSION BY JAMES JILER, HSNY

example, that people leaving jail or prison tend to move to core areas of impoverishment where housing and services are affordable. In New York

GreenHouse operates under the premise
that jail can serve as a sustainable
resource—one that generates benefits
to constituents in jail as well as to entire
communities across the city and region.

Manhattan rooftop garden
built and installed by
GreenTeam members.
PHOTO USED WITH PERMISSION
BY JAMES JILER, HSNY

City, 70 percent of the 16,000 inmates on Rikers come from five core neighborhoods — East New York, Crown Heights, Bushwick, South Bronx and East Harlem (Wynn 2001). The opportunities and influences found in this setting will statistically determine whether an ex-offender will return to jail within 1 year of release (Petersilia 2003).

HSNY's GreenTeam is the "street" arm of our jail-to-street program and provides an avenue of support for inmates leaving jail.Inmates with an interest in horticulture can begin working with the GreenTeam as paid interns the day they arrive home, earning $7.50 to $10 per hour while honing their skills for a future career in the "greening" field. The program's salary and skill-building is comparable to that of an income-generating landscape/gardening firm. As long as there are contracts, HSNY can afford to retain and pay interns to carry out the work. Some of our contracts take place in luxury buildings, penthouses, or private homes. But the focus of HSNY's income-generating projects is on partnerships with community-based organizations and service providers. These may be schools, psychiatric institutions, facilities that provide residential services to the mentally ill, people with HIV, at-risk youth, family shelters, seniors, and the disabled. The work may consist of planting street trees, building rooftop gardens, installing specialty gardens for food, herbs, or gardens strictly for therapeutic activities. Not only does the process involve former inmates, but clients of the community based organizations are also active participants, becoming — as their skills and knowledge develop — stewards of the resident garden. As both ex-offenders and clients assume control of resources they had no prior connection to, they begin to assume a measure of **control** over their lives. It is a realization that success is dependent on the role they take in managing the sites, and how that role is played out on a daily basis of work and dialogue.

→ SEE MURPHY-DUNNING
PAGE 154

Over time, the number of gardens and projects and people involved add up to a green continuum among neighborhoods and communities. It begins at Rikers, where the individual learns the simple connection between work, responsibility, care and the benefits associated with cultivating not just the garden, but themselves. It continues as ex-offenders who, for the most part are marginalized from mainstream society, leave Rikers with the ability to immerse themselves in professional gardening work. This not only gives them vital skills to find and hold a job, but extends their influence to developing meaningful spaces in areas ranging from wealthy neighborhoods to low-income, under-served communities. It may be a neighborhood branch library garden, or a strip of park land on the Hudson River, or a street tree in a hot zone of Hunts Point, Bronx. And the beginning has no end; we've found that garden-work sensibilities extend to families and children, neighbors, and parents. I think of Martin C., one of my first students on Rikers in 1997, who planted his first garden during his incarceration. During 10 years he held jobs ranging from seasonal work as a zoo horticulturist at the Prospect Park Zoo, to a full-time zone gardener in Central Park, to the establishment of his own small lawn-care business in Long Island. In 2007, Martin's son, Martin Jr., joined the GreenTeam, not as an ex-offender, but as part of the program's expansion and outreach to "at-risk" youth.

Over the past year and now planning into the future, the GreenHouse and GreenTeam are reaching out to adolescents in jail and upon return to their neighborhoods, under the assumption that work skills and meaningful work are preventative measures that can break the rate of incarceration among at-risk youth. In the mid-1980s, The HSNY established a vocational horticulture program for adolescent boys that was supported through a city-based Youth Service Grant. In 1994, the grant was terminated and the program — then called GreenWorks — folded. When HSNY returned to Rikers in 1997, the focus was on men and women adults, primarily because adolescents were mandated to attend school during the day. Now, however, with re-entry and rehabilitation taking a strong role in the ever-shifting criminal justice paradigm, jails such as Rikers are revisiting the importance of vocational skill development for youth offenders. A unique aspect of the program that GreenHouse provides is the "street" component — the opportunity for men, women, and youth to continue a vocation that they started in jail.

While the program has shown measured success in reducing recidivism among its participants (25 percent as compared to 65 percent of the Rikers population) the stark reality is GreenHouse, and programs like GreenHouse are under-utilized as an alternative to modern incarceration practices. The potential of this program — at Rikers and in facilities across the country — could be more fully realized by increasing the resources devoted to alternative programs rather than solely focusing on inmate control. In her book, "When Prisoners Come Home," Joan Petersilia states that just "one-third of all prisoners released will have received vocational or educational training." In California alone, of 132,000 inmates released in 2002, just 8,000 received some kind of aftercare support to help them successfully reenter and remain in their community (Jiler 2006). At Rikers, GreenHouse provides services to less than 25 inmates daily; and only 1 to 2 percent of the Rikers Island total population of approximately 15,000 inmates are eligible to participate in the program. Overall, GreenHouse could accommodate far more inmates, and provide more opportunities to rehabilitate inmates with meaningful work skills in gardening, horticulture, and environmental restoration and management. With the cost of constructing new prisons averaging well over $70,000 per cell, and the yearly cost of incarcerating an inmate averaging $50,000, horticulture programs are a low-cost alternative to punitive measures of imprisonment.

One year out of jail, William R. takes his son to water his plot in a **community garden** on 9th Street in Manhattan. Since his release, he → SEE STONE PAGE 122 has worked steadily with the GreenTeam, has become a certified tree climber and readily dispenses gardening advice to an inquiring public on 9th Street. Is William a success story? Occasionally he relapses into alcohol and drug use, which prevents him from holding a steady job in the profession. But unlike before, a relapse is less likely to end in jail than in the garden. For William, horticulture is a lifeline that keeps him on a forward path, despite a history of jail and substance abuse.

"You may not see changes," he tells me. "But I know I'm changing. I'm doing things differently."

When he's not working as a gardener, William is on 9th street, gardening for the fun of it.

On its own, horticulture is not a panacea for the huge challenges facing the criminal justice system either in New York City, the state, or country. With almost 2 million men and women serving time behind bars nationally, up to 600,000 are released each year returning to their communities with weak prospects for the future. Up to 80 percent are in for drug related crimes and a high percentage have serious addictions or mental illness. Many former inmates are simply not healthy enough to work a 40-hour week in horticulture, nor can they cope with the serious issues confronting them after their release from jail.

Programs such as GreenHouse must work hand in hand with other nonprofits that target substance abuse, housing, trauma, physical health and mental health issues as well as job training in fields unrelated to gardening. It must partner with community groups such as Sustainable South Bronx or **Added Value in Red Hook**, Brooklyn that have their own "green" job training component for neighborhood youth. It must act as a model for other jurisdictions that hope to replicate similar programs for their criminal justice system. And to generate success, it most focus on its students, one individual, and one garden at a time.

→ SEE MARVY PAGE 202

Prior to her arrest and incarceration at Rikers, Kamelita, now 28 years old, moved from job to job with little ambition or idea of developing a professional career. With two small children and no high school diploma she was mostly concerned with paying rent, putting food on the table, and her children's education. She spent 6 months with GreenTeam and was an intern at the Brooklyn Botanic Garden before landing her job with a private firm as a plant technician. Today, she will quickly tell you that horticulture is her life with opportunities branching out like a fast growing tree. "I have private clients, and plenty of overtime and the trust from my boss that I'll always leave a site in perfect condition," she said. More important, Kamelita is part of the greater collective of gardeners greening New York.

"Everyday I'm doing this," she said, "I feel that I'm getting paid to give something back to the community."

The feeling is not limited to Kamelita: it is something that germinates in many of the men and women we work with in jail and with some care, develops into positive behavior that leaves in its wake a healthy, more livable city for themselves, and for everyone else.

Dialogue With Author:
Are there any precedents that informed your work? Or similar projects like yours? Or is it wholly unique?

There are many horticulture programs in jails and prisons throughout the country, but none that offer a jail-to-street continuum. I personally was inspired by Catherine Sneed's work in San Francisco. Not only did she start a large-scale organic farm on jail grounds but found a vacant lot in the city for released inmates to gather, garden, and stay positive. Later, she established a contract with the Department of Public Works that provided work for ex-offenders to plant and maintain street trees in San Francisco. While her gardening program in jail and her work for ex-offenders planting trees no longer has the funding to support itself, as a model it continues to inform and inspire (see Jiler 2006).

My predecessor at HSNY, Arthur Sheppard who started GreenWorks – a program that worked with adolescent males on Rikers – and later established an early incarnation of GreenTeam, was equally influential. GreenHouse is simply a second-generation version of GreenWork that was expanded to include men and women adults. We then privatized GreenTeam (under Arthur the GreenTeam was supported by foundation grants) by seeking contracts to generate income. This created a large measure of financial sustainability and support for the program

John Cannizzo, the current Director of GreenTeam also deserves much credit for his work expanding the program, building partnerships with different groups across the city, and reaching out to include at-risk youth through Federation Employment and Guidance Service, Inc. (FEGS) and Graham-Windham, (an organization that works with youth graduating from foster care). This job-training component adds a whole new dimension to our mission of establishing a generation of professional stewards dedicated to improving environmental and human health in their communities.

Literature Cited

Elsner, A. 2004. **Gates of injustice.** Upper Saddle River, NJ: Prentice Hall.

Jiler, J. 2006. **Doing time in the garden.** Oakland, CA: New Village Press.

Petersilia, J. 2003. **When prisoners come home.** New York, NY: Oxford University Press.

Wynn, J. 2001. **Inside Rikers.** New York, NY: St. Martins Press.

Memoryscape

Lindsay Campbell
U.S. Forest Service, Northern Research Station

The Brian Joseph Murphy Memorial Preservation Land, Westfield, MA

Site Description

Shade tobacco fields, an abandoned train overpass, dense trees, dirt roads, hawks, deer, and even the occasional moose. These are features in the one-time "romping grounds" of Brian Joseph Murphy, Harold Murphy, and many other children of Westfield, MA — the place known as "100 acres" that is now permanently preserved under the Winding Rivers Land Trust. Harold Murphy worked with three local businessmen to preserve over 30 acres of open space in memory of his brother Brian, who was killed at the World Trade Center on September 11, 2001 (9-11). Harold is a real estate developer with experience in open space conservation and a deep commitment to the historic preservation of his rural, western Massachusetts community. Both he and his brother had a prior interest in preserving this piece of property that was owned by longtime Westfield resident and personal friend, Dick Fowler. After Brian's death, when an opportunity emerged to purchase the property, several friends and associates of Harold and Brian insisted that they do so in Brian's name.

For both aesthetic and sentimental reasons, this land is sacred to Harold and other Westfield residents. The stream, trestle, and patch of woodland are surrounded almost entirely by functioning farms and it takes a four wheel drive or a pair of boots to access this beautiful, hidden landscape. It is a place where kids come for parties, romance, isolation, and other excitement, immersed in densely vegetated nature. As Harold and Brian did in their youth, the current teenagers of Westfield continue to use the land as a wild refuge, a place of privacy out of the watchful eye of parents and a world apart from the everyday expectations of school, home, and community. The site was also the place where Harold and Brian, as adults, would go to catch up when

Brian would visit from New York City. Harold discussed his history with
the site:

> "I do consider it sacred, but I guess I always have. As a kid, you come upon
> times when you really need to be by yourself because nobody loves you or
> whatever. This is where I would come and sit on the edge of the bridge and
> think about life and [ask] 'should you fall or not?' You come to your own grips
> with things. But I know if I come down here and walk around, I'm recharged
> and I know that the world is good and life is going to go on. I can hear my
> friends' voices and see the playing around we did down here as little kids.
> I feel it, very strongly."

The natural beauty of the site and the personal memories he holds from
growing up in that landscape are what make it sacred. He continues to
use the site as a place for quiet walks and family visits, both with his
8-year-old daughter, as well as Brian's widow and two children. Harold
has struggled with depression since Brian's death. Brian's children,
in response to the loss of their father on 9-11, have been coping with

Harold Murphy
PHOTO USED WITH PERMISSION
BY PHOTOGRAPHER IAN CHENEY

delayed onset stress reactions, which makes having a place to go to "center their emotions" that much more important, according to Harold. The family refers to the site as "Brian's land" and takes comfort simply in knowing that it exists, in "knowing that their dad had a *place*." Right now, there is no signage or marker to indicate that the land is a memorial. No one but the family and a few neighbors know the intent of this preservation land; in some ways it is really a private memorial space in the public domain. The site is not used for formal remembrance or ceremony. Instead, it is a space to create positive new memories, while being enveloped by fond older memories that are imbued in that place.

In terms of future use of the forest, the land will remain in a state very similar to its current condition. A landscape architect was consulted on this project, and he advised Harold and the land trust to simply "leave it alone" because of the natural beauty of the site. It will not likely be farmed again, though wild asparagus may continue to grow. The adjacent tobacco farm is still active. The only notable difference in the landscape is a set of housing developments on the bluff overlooking the back portion of the lands, allowing the residents a prized, wooded viewshed. A planned rail-trail will eventually bring active recreation through the site in the form of walkers, runners, and bicyclers. The only aspect of the site that may be developed as more of a built memorial will be three granite benches with the names of Westfield's deceased on 9-11, and stone monuments to "justice, peace, mercy, and love", which — according to a Hebrew creation tale — are the attributes that brought the world out of chaos. These built monuments will be adjacent to a planned peace and teaching garden to be created and maintained by area schoolchildren, to help teach values of stewardship and nature.

Landscape as Memorial

Landscape can support human health not only through direct biophysical services and benefits, but also through social functions that — while sometimes subtle and not easy to detect — remain vital to the health of individuals and communities. Open space and natural resources are often used in acts of memorialization, acts of marking or designating land in memory of individuals or events. These accessible materials of the natural world become vehicles for expression, or ways of "gaining authorship", in Harold Murphy's words. Furthermore, across many cultures and eras, sacred trees and groves have been used in rituals connected to the lifecycle (Rival 1999). In the context of the contemporary United States, trees and gardens have been planted and parks and forests have been dedicated as memorials in honor of a number of events of national significance, such as World War I, World War II, and more recently 9-11. The Living Memorials Project was created by the Forest Service at the direction of U.S. Congress immediately following 9-11. The Living Memorials Project consisted of a grants program aimed at supporting communities and stewardship groups in the creation of landscape-based living memorials, as well as a multi-year research project to understand changes in the use of natural resources in response to 9-11. Through that research, which was directed by Erika Svendsen and me, I came to recognize some of the deeply sacred ways in which landscape is used as memorial space and healing space. The Brian Joseph Murphy Memorial Preservation Land is just one of the 700 memorials that we documented and the 150 groups that we interviewed.

When thinking of 9-11 memorials, much attention is given to New York City, the Pentagon, and Shanksville, PA, where the physical crash sites are located and where memorials aimed at national audiences will eventually be created. However, the living memorials research revealed a powerful, dispersed network of community-based memorials that spans the country and occurs in all sorts of site types, embedded in the everyday landscape. The Westfield, Massachusetts site of Brian Joseph Murphy's memorial does not have any immediate or significant geographic connection to New York City, but Westfield was Brian's hometown, and he was living in New York City and working at the World Trade Center at the time of 9-11. These sorts of invisible social networks became more apparent and readable through the landscape following the tragedy of that day. Families, friends, and communities, marked their lawns, schoolyards, parks, and town greens with memorials. Clusters of 9-11 memorials are apparent in the Boston area — from which two of the planes departed — and in the Los Angeles area — where two of the planes were originally destined. Other clusters exist along commuter corridors in New Jersey and Long Island, as well as in retirement communities in southern Florida, and the Virginia and Maryland suburbs of Washington, D.C. (Svendsen and Campbell 2006).

Adjacent land uses:
shade tobacco farms
and a bicycle plant.
PHOTOS BY LINDSAY CAMPBELL,
U.S. FOREST SERVICE, NORTHERN
RESEARCH STATION

A small river winds
through the site.
PHOTO BY LINDSAY CAMPBELL,
U.S. FOREST SERVICE, NORTHERN
RESEARCH STATION

The abandoned train
trestle will be converted
into a hike-bike trail.
PHOTO BY LINDSAY CAMPBELL,
U.S. FOREST SERVICE, NORTHERN
RESEARCH STATION

This forest is not the only memorial to Brian in Westfield. Harold showed the Living Memorials Project researchers two other sites in town: a picnic pavilion at the Sons of Erin (an Irish American social club) dedicated to the three residents of Westfield that were lost; and a prayer garden at the Genesis House church. Harold said,

"It's very bittersweet to come down and see the memorials. To be quite honest, a lot of times you don't want to come and see them. But, it's good. It is good. You need to remember."

Though he is both touched by and proud of these memorials, Harold noted that he is not able to visit these memorials very often, they are simply too painful as reminders of his loss. The same is true to an even greater degree with the Ground Zero site. Although Harold goes back every year on Sept. 11 and some other occasions, it is a deeply emotional and painful trip to make. "It's a good thing and a bad thing to go," Harold said. Not only did Harold suffer the trauma of losing his brother on that day, but also he was a direct witness to the event; he was at Ground Zero when Building 7 collapsed, surrounded by military, paramilitary, and police forces — memories that flood back and return to him in layers any time he visits the city. Harold does not even have to visit the site to be reminded of his loss; images of the New York City skyline, or the Twin Towers, are replayed in the media and repeated throughout the quotidian human terrain of diners, gas stations, and bumper stickers. His personal loss is part of the shared grief of the nation.

The subsequent design debates and real estate deals that have unfolded at the World Trade Center site have left Harold frustrated and alienated. Along with many other 9-11 family members, Harold believes that the site is sacred, hallowed ground that should never be developed and should be left as passive, open space. He noted that we would never think to build office space and skyscrapers atop Civil War battlefields; but there are no American precedents for a terrorist act of this scale in such an urban center. Furthermore, he finds the claims of "balance" between development and memorial uncompelling. In this case, there is no middle ground for him — "you either do the right thing or you don't." The competing interests and desires for the site set up an almost intractable planning problem. It is no wonder, then, that family members and friends of victims, even in the immediate New York City area, turned to their own backyards and communities to create sacred places to honor the memory of the deceased. In this way, family members are able to have a meaningful voice in where and how their loved ones are remembered. Thus, memorials are sites for those who live on, though they are created in the name of the deceased. This is — perhaps counter-intuitively — as much Harold's memorial as it is Brian's.

The Stewardship of Memory

Just like thousands of other family members, Harold Murphy devoted much of his life immediately following the tragedy of 9-11 to the public and private remembrance of his deceased loved one. Many families, including Brian's family, were deprived of the traditional rites of burial due to the fact that bodies were not recovered for many of the victims. These same family members were simultaneously thrust into contentious decisions about public funding, land use changes, and memorial design at the national memorial sites. Therefore, it is important to study the memorials that family members chose to take part in creating, maintaining, or using — sites that they embrace as "their own" — to try and understand at least some aspects of the memorial, healing, and recovery processes. The physical sites that family members establish and transform into living memorials will remain as legacies for the future, from unmarked open space, to parkland, to formal sites of remembrance. The ways in which they choose to remember their loved ones are often clear reflections of the ways they live their lives. The memorials are shaped by the physical places, social networks, and value systems of family members, other stewards, and their communities.

As a steward of the land trust and a resident of Westfield, Harold himself is personally invested and deeply committed. Even in its current, overgrown state, Harold enjoys walking the railroad right-of-way from the center of Westfield out to Brian's land. He observes the section as it progresses from commercial center, to residential areas, to former industrial sites, to agricultural land, to woods, providing a tangible, physical connection between his everyday landscape, the history of the community, and the forest. He described his personal history with the site in a narrative interwoven with the history of the town. His family moved to Westfield directly from Ireland in the mid-1800s. In 1904, his

grandmother bought the family homestead that is still in use today. With deep family roots in this small town, he refers to immigration waves, industrial shifts, past residents, infamous tales, and changes in land ownership in rich detail. For Harold, the memorial land takes its meaning not only from its beauty or ecosystem function, but from the way in which people interact with it — in this case from the Irish immigrant families, to the Jamaican and Mexican farm workers on the shade tobacco fields, to the current children of Westfield. Beyond Westfield, Harold is embedded in the entire western Massachusetts landscape. He can describe back roads in vivid visual detail; the act of giving directions becomes both an opportunity for storytelling and a history lesson. He relished the opportunity to describe beautiful vistas, winding roads, and to take this researcher to a local maple sugar shack.

Harold has also come to appreciate one of the greatest functions that environmental stewardship can serve through his local volunteer work with Parent Leadership Training Institute (PLTI). He serves on the board of this social service organization that supports underserved populations by offering leadership training and organizational support for participant-led community building projects. As **Erika Svendsen** → SEE SVENDSEN PAGE 58 argues in this volume, the need to create or control at least some aspect of one's life (particularly given that much of it is beyond our control) can often come to be articulated through the landscape. Harold shared an anecdote of a severely abused woman (who came to PLTI) who compulsively cleaned and rearranged her home throughout the time of the abuse, as it was the only means through which she could assert that control. Others express this same need in the landscape, through acts such as tree planting, mural making, memorial creation, and community gardening. Indeed, half of the projects that are proposed and enacted by PLTI participants during the 20-week leadership program are efforts that involve community stewardship of natural resources, including tree planting, community gardens, and neighborhood beautification projects. Harold believes that the parent participants are motivated to improve the physical environment in which they raise their children. Natural resources are accessible, all around us, and are vehicles for self-expression as individuals and a collective.

Lindsay Campbell interviewing Harold Murphy, walking on the train right-of-way.
PHOTO USED WITH PERMISSION BY PHOTOGRAPHER IAN CHENEY

Reflection

There is something special in this wooded landscape. For all of my appreciation of urbanity, community gardens, urban forests, and neighborhood greening, each time I visit this rather rural site I am forced to reckon with its beauty, its visceral emotional presence. Perhaps this is simply my experience of **biophilia**; the treed slopes surrounding the railroad right-of-way create protected, linear sightlines; the running water creates a pleasant white noise; the vivid red blossoms of the sumac draw my attention and the fuzzy branches invite human touch. And the rusting railway trestle reminds of "the necessity of ruins," as J.B. Jackson (1980) said. Not only the individual features, but the orientation of the site — off a dirt road, sandwiched between the back sides of properties — gives it a protected and isolated feel, despite its small size. As such, the site encourages Westfield youth to engage in the unstructured, naturalistic play that Richard Louv (2006) so prizes in his book "Last Child in the Woods." It seems that what creates a "Restorative Commons" from a physical, landscape design perspective is site specific; it is difficult to analyze, package, or export to other sites. But what captivates my attention and stirs such emotion in me is my ability to see the site through Harold's eyes, as a place of both respite and adventure. To hear of his passionate love for his community and the deep, shared memories embedded in a site is to understand "place attachment" in a nonconceptual way. Indeed, in the words of Stephen J. Gould, "We cannot win this battle to save species and environments without forging an emotional bond between ourselves and nature as well — for we will not fight to save what we do not love" (Gould 1991).

→ SEE HEERWAGEN PAGE 38

While unique sites cannot be replicated or transposed, sound stewardship can be cultivated. Harold's passionate care for the landscape stems from positive and interactive experiences with it, suggesting a role for environmental educators, community groups, and natural resource managers. The story of experiences in nature can be told and retold — both passed down to children and shared with peers, with the implied call to go out and create our own experiences in the landscape. Harold's act of storytelling, his invitation to see the land through his eyes, is truly a "living memorial" to his brother and one with more humanity and emotion than any plaque fixed to the ground.

Furthermore, as issues such as climate change continue to increase in urgency and in the public awareness, it is important to think of natural resources holistically. Trees are not simply carbon sinks; gardens are not simply opportunities to retain urban storm water. Certainly they provide these important biophysical services, but they also shape our lived experience of a place. Landscape shapes our memories, our preferences, and aspects of our culture. And Harold's valuation and memories of his childhood and lifelong home motivated him to help preserve that legacy for future generations.

This environmental stewardship ethic is rooted in a deeply personal experience of place, rather than an abstract value of "nature." Though he is a real estate developer or perhaps because he is a developer, Harold understands the importance of public open space and wants the land to remain whole and accessible to people rather than carved into lots for private and exclusive use. All of his current development projects now have strong conservation requirements in which common lands are set aside as open space to be managed by a private nonprofit made up of landowners. Another legacy that this site is leaving is through the way in which it may inspire other future residents to join in the preservation effort. "It really galvanized people to think about what we could put together and what we could save," said Harold. "We got a lot of good local press and people are coming forward and saying 'I have land we'd like to preserve.'"

Literature Cited

Gould, Stephen Jay. 1991. Unenchanted evening. Natural History. 100(9).

Jackson, J.B. 1980. The necessity for ruins. Amherst, MA: University of Massachusetts Press. 129 p.

Louv, R. 2006. Last child in the woods: saving our children from nature deficit disorder. Chapel Hill, NC: Algonquin Books of Chapel Hill. 323 p.

Rival, L., ed. 1999. The social life of trees: anthropological perspectives on tree symbolism. Oxford, UK: Berg. 315 p.

Svendsen, E; Campbell, L. 2006. Land-markings: 12 journeys through 9/11 Living Memorials. NRS-INF-1-06. Newtown Square, PA: U.S. Department of Agriculture, Forest Service, Northern Research Station. 49 p.

To hear of his passionate love for his community and the deep, shared memories embedded in a site is to understand "place attachment" in a nonconceptual way.

Interviews

Interviews were conducted with practitioners building Restorative Commons in diverse landscapes — from Brooklyn to Sarajevo. We hear practitioners' voices, learn their views, and investigate their commonly shared and worked spaces that catalyze social ties, healthful habitats, and human potential. Views expressed by interviewees are their own and do not necessarily reflect views of the other authors, of Meristem, or of the U.S. Forest Service. We hope that their perspectives and insights inspire response, debate, and new Restorative Commons.

Youth Empowerment through Urban Agriculture: Red Hook Community Farm

Interview with Ian Marvy
Added Value, Brooklyn, NY

Lindsay Campbell: What is the main goal of Added Value and the Red Hook Community Farm?

What we're trying to do here is create a more sustainable world; the way we want to do that is through youth empowerment and urban agriculture. We are taking public space that was programmed for one use, one economy, and one social structure, and transforming it into something else. What we believe we're doing as an organization and a learning community is transforming what was a 20th century park into a 21st century park — literally a public commons.

What a 21st century park means to us is that we can use a public space to educate people about a truly democratic process: how to care about social issues. We can provide them with skills development and training to help build that world, while simultaneously building an economic process that nurtures the community and nurtures the environment. It doesn't just lessen the ills that we've done. This is a project that harvests waste from the surroundings to generate nutrients, to generate ideas and energy. Often when we think about our work, we talk about words like: catalytic, inspirational, transformative, community.

I'm not really interested in any of my teens becoming farmers. What I care about is that they grow up caring. They know they're cared for. They know that caring matters. They have skills to help them articulate that and actualize that in terms of building a more caring world. Hopefully they can share that with other people. That's what this kind of space and this kind of program can do.

Previous Page:
Youth working at Red Hook Farm, Brooklyn, NY.
PHOTO USED WITH PERMISSION BY ADDED VALUE

Left:
Ian Marvy teaches composting with youth visitors to the farm.
PHOTO USED WITH PERMISSION BY ADDED VALUE

Anne Wiesen: I think I understand your vision of a 21st century park, but what do you mean by a 20th century park?

The public playground movement in the United States began out of Clark College and was focused on child development and related to the new immigration at the turn of the last century. The first head of the American Playground Association was involved with the development of most of the public parks here in New York City — the playgrounds,

→ SEE MARTENSEN PAGE 26

not the large-scale parks like Van Courtland, **Central Park**, Prospect Park — we're talking about the parks that the vast majority of working class people use. Those parks were designed as places to get the poor out of their tenements, get them physically active, and get them healthy. They were also talked about as citizenship projects and *civilizing* projects. Sandboxes were a place where children returned to primordial soup. Then they progressed to small ball games and little climbing structures so that children could develop their own relationship with the built environment. That then moved onto shared games and play — sports activities. Those sports activities were primarily written about as citizenship cultivation, and in particular citizens in a 20th century economic order. So, you needed to learn how to play the left fullback or the third baseman or whatever it was because you needed to know where to pop a rivet. You needed to know where you would be in the economic order. You needed to know how to follow rules, team play, and how your play contributed to the overall good as defined by those in charge. What we're sitting on here was a baseball field and a football field that was flooded in the winter to become an ice skating rink.

LC: Why the name Added Value?

Added Value took its name from the system of energy transfer that begins with the sun and creates energy that go into plants that are then harvested by animals of all different varieties and then reharvested by decomposers, and that whole cycle. Unfortunately, what's very unique about human beings is that we have to choose to "add value" to that cycle. We have created ourselves as extractive people that pull away from that system. We've built a society and an economy that drag resources out of that cycle. What Michael Hurwitz and I want to suggest is that we could inspire people to make the choice to add value by working with teens and working with food.

LC: So, why focus on urban agriculture?

Food is something every person has a connection to and young people are something that everybody has a connection to. And often both of them are things that people have strong opinions about, they care about them.

    Prior to running Added Value I was doing a **restorative justice** project with Michael Hurwitz, working with first time youth offenders in a community garden. One day I pulled a dandelion green out of the ground and got into a long discussion with a teenager about culturally appropriate food — he wasn't interested. Healthy eating — he wasn't interested. Good cooking — he wasn't interested. He wasn't interested in any of the typical models of education and inspiration that we might deal with. What he was interested in was growing dandelion greens in a 10 foot x 10 foot space and selling his produce at a $1.75/pound. I told him — hypothetically — he could make $75 on this space of land for very little investment. Then I talked to him about what would it mean to grow dandelion roots instead of dandelion greens. Dandelion root is a medicinal plant that supports kidney and liver function. So, we grow roots for a year, clean them off, chop them up, soak them in alcohol, and let them cure for a year. And at the same time we do some education in the community about our own health and wellness. And then we turn around and in the same plot of land we have $1,200 worth of dandelion

→ SEE JILER PAGE 178

Teen participants work the farmers market.
PHOTO USED WITH PERMISSION BY PHIL SHIPMAN, ADDED VALUE

What a 21st century park means to us is
that we can use a public space to educate
people about a truly democratic process:
how to care about social issues. We can…
build an economic process that nutures the
community and nurtures the environment.

Red Hook Farm
PHOTO USED WITH PERMISSION
BY PHIL SHIPMAN, ADDED VALUE

root tincture that we can sell below market value to our neighbors. Now, this kid's no dummy, his family sells heroin and he knows what economic systems look like. He knows what supply and demand look like. And he knows what health and lack of health look like. He asked me for a job doing exactly what we had just discussed, but I didn't have a job to give him. At that point, Added Value did not exist.

LC: How did you identify your site?

→ SEE BENNATON PAGE 232

We were working in a **New York City Housing Authority** community garden, and we knew that that wasn't going to be enough space. And we were running a farmers' market in a park not far from here. I was walking out to lunch with, Ben Balcolm, one of the farmers from our market and we walked past this site. I lived in the neighborhood, but I had never been here. It was a dilapidated, unused park. Ben said, "That's a great urban farm. You've got nice wind here, a nice wind break, you've got great southern exposure, a 12-foot fence, 2.5 to 3 acres, and it doesn't look like anything's going on there." Then we went off to lunch. I came back here and crawled through the fence and totally cried in the middle of the field. It was so much fun. I was like, "This is sweet!"

AW: Was the decision to build raised beds of soil on top of the asphalt out of concern for health or liability?

It was an economic decision at the time. This is formerly a railroad change yard for the docking station, which — relatively speaking — is a nontoxic use as far as industry goes. It's just to change cars. It wasn't a loading and unloading facility. So, relatively speaking, it was a clean site compared to the brownfields that are all around us. We've got 5 inches of cement and at that time Added Value had a budget of about $5,000. Tearing up the cement would have cost $140,000 and I can get compost for free.

LC: Who do you target with your programs?

The core of our work has always been teenagers. That's in large part because that's what Michael and I did for 10 years before we started Added Value, both of us were youth workers. The staff that we have hired are also all primarily youth workers. Typically 17 to 20 teens are somehow involved in the project.

How does the history of Red Hook shape your current work?

This park was built in an immigrant, Irish and Italian, neighborhood. Those Irish and Italian families worked out here on the docks when there were 50,000 families living in this neighborhood and probably more working in it. The docks did two things: they either brought food from the other world, primarily bulk products; or they built and rebuilt the boats that were doing that work or supporting the colonial endeavors of the 20th century.

With a few major public policy decisions in this neighborhood, city, and state, this community was killed. The city decided not to have maritime industry be part of its economic future, and obviously that was the economy that was here. Simultaneously, Robert Moses was involved with his design projects, which included the Brooklyn-Queens Expressway and the Brooklyn Battery Tunnel. These were constructed at the same time and cut the neighborhood off from the rest of the community leading to the destruction of the economic engine and the physical isolation of the neighborhood.

Then you had the GI Bill—essentially a Marshall Plan for the United States. You send all these people off to war and they come back traumatized. The economy had been entirely oriented toward the manufacturing of weapons and the food to feed people, and that economy was going to collapse. So we gave all these people housing loans, which meant they were going to build houses and we gave them free college—so those who couldn't get involved in the manufacturing industry building houses could go off to college and become teachers. It was an incredible asset to the country. But the military was segregated. So what we remember as the GI Bill was a massive transfer of wealth to white, working class people. It was a great thing; it was also disproportionate and created a large wealth gap. So the vast majority of the

white community began to leave Red Hook to go off to Long Island to places where they could build homes and go off to college. So within a matter of 16 years, from 1947 to 1963, this community was gutted and left to suffer through urban blight.

In 1962 you started to see real urban decay coupled with urban renewal projects almost immediately. Essentially what you had in Red Hook in the late 1980s and early '90s is a community of 10,000 people, 8,400 of whom are living in public housing, with an average income of $12,000 for a family of four, which is half of the poverty line in New York City. So, amid that context, Added Value was formed out of concern about the way people were approaching Red Hook—defining its opportunities externally. There were all sorts of other people's dreams for this neighborhood. But without access to capital or education and a pro-social agenda that would allow people to make changes in their lives, all of those plans failed. They failed for a number of reasons, but primarily because they didn't help people *here* get educated, get involved, and improve their lives.

An adaptive strategy:
building raised beds on top
of the asphalt ballfield.
PHOTO USED WITH PERMISSION
BY ADDED VALUE

Seed-to-Salad participant
in the 2nd grade,
harvesting the lettuce she
planted. Each spring, first-
and second-grade students
participate in this 10-week
program, sowing seeds
in April, harvesting and
eating a salad in June,
and learning about plants,
food, and farm life cycles.
PHOTO USED WITH PERMISSION
BY JENNIE ALLEN

LC: What is your involvement with schools?

We work very intensively with three elementary schools. In the spring we work with 120 elementary school students for an hour and a half per week for 10 weeks on the farm. We work with Food Change with another 80 elementary school students on a 22-week, 3 hour/week curricula. We do an hour and a half in the classroom and an hour and a half on the farm.

PS 15 is the school we do the intensive program with, and we got a call from Trust for Public Land (TPL) this spring that said, "We have a problem." TPL has their commons project where they get large grants to develop NYC Department of Education playgrounds into more community-friendly places through a participatory design process with the kids in the schools and input from the community. I ask, "What's the problem?" They said, "Well, the first-, second-, and third-graders are voting in a bloc for greenspace on the playground. They're voting for greenhouses, butterfly bushes, edible food gardens. More than a stage to perform on, more than a badminton court, more than a tennis court, more than a running track." So, given a choice, given the opportunity to participate actively in the design of their environment, children who were exposed to an inquiry-based farm and food learning experience were choosing the 21st century experience. They were choosing to have a garden where they could continue the inquiry, learning about seasons and cycles. So TPL had to change the design and we had to come to some compromises and say that we would help support it. A lot of the barriers are familiar: staffing, maintenance. It's harder to keep up a garden than it is to keep up a cement football field. It takes different resources.

AW: What is the relationship between your urban farm, other farms in the region, and global food sources?

Currently I don't think a fully local system works. I think an *ethic of localizing* might work. So, for example, we run a farmers' market. We don't just sell our own urban stuff because that wouldn't feed the needs of the community. And in some sense, it would not be able to have the impact that it does. But with four other farmers in the region dropping off their products, we get to build an urban-rural linkage. We get to recognize that an apple from Red Hook, New York — which is 60 miles from here — is better than an apple from Washington state, which is better than apple juice from China — which is *ridiculous*.

AW: Would you tell us about the systemic impact of the farm at the neighborhood scale?

We've done a waste audit; we can handle a lot of compost here, a lot more than we have now. We take about 100 five-gallon buckets a week from one restaurant. We've just started what will hopefully be an all-urban Community Supported Agriculture (CSA). The CSA gets picked up in a 5-gallon bucket, you bring it home, the food scraps get brought back in the bucket, and then you get a new bucket. Also, we work with three local restaurants, and all three of restaurants in this neighborhood are owned by people in this neighborhood. They purchase food from a not-for-profit in this neighborhood that hires teens through an internship program and pays those teens to grow food in the neighborhood. So a dollar spent at one of these restaurants stays in the neighborhood four times — or some portion of that dollar.

Economic and environmental systems like that used to exist everywhere and, by and large, they still exist in a lot of the world. But they exist less and less. Globalized economies hurt the purpose of the commons. They pull away from the commons. But having an economy where my children know the restaurateurs who buy their stuff, they can say hello to them on the street — that's a truly local economy. So that's the macro-vision, we do that right now. That's *common*-ality, that's common-*unity*, that's community, that's where it goes.

LC: You're *clearly* deeply committed to Red Hook as a neighborhood. Do you ever see yourself trying to replicate this model in other places?

We are replicating by example. There are 12,000 people here and I would rather personally know each one of them and have each one of them know the farm. That's just my personal bent. Institutionally, we're growing so fast and that growth is really about meeting the need right here. It wouldn't make any sense to try and replicate in other places.

Across the country, I think we're seeing groups like Added Value more and more. There was a reason that Added Value was a very unique organization 7 years ago, but we're a very un-unique organization now.

That's common-ality, that's common-unity, that's community, that's where it goes.

AW: What would your ideal vision be if you had the funds and had the choice about how to grow the farm?

We had a design charrette for the farm to think about what the farm would look like and, we're also going through a participatory strategic planning process. Heifer is leading it in large part because of, 1) their long-term understanding of the organizations successes and challenges; and 2) their holistic approach, which could be likened to whole-farm planning or whole-planning. It's very integrated. And the hope is that that will help us develop a 3 to 5 year plan.

Currently, the conceptual plan is to have a 4,000-square-foot building in the northwest corner, bermed under soil in the back and open facing due south, with classroom space, food processing space, and office space there. About 4,000 feet of greenhouse space with an integrated aquaponic system and growing environment. A 2,000-square-foot barn for small ruminants — chickens and rabbits. And then, a large-scale community composting facility in about 100,000 feet and another outdoor classroom kind of space. **Bioswales**, all the **groundwater and graywater** gets treated on site. A windmill on site. Its easy for that kind of building, we only need 47kw/h. We've done this whole survey, I can operate off of wind and sun here. But we'll put in a biofuel processor and a diesel boiler on site so we can be triple redundant. We should be totally off the grid. And, again, it's a citizenship project. It's not a farm or a classroom. All that has to be interpretable and interactive. You've got to be able to touch it, see it, feel it. As a first-grader — we have to have lessons to help them "get" power. You can't just have a windmill, that's boring.

Beyond the farm site, the Red Hook Houses is one of the greenest public housing developments in the city. Greenspace per person is quite high over there. I would *love* to build a farm there. I would *love* at some point for somebody to say, "Hey, instead of coming over here and buying my greens, why don't we take the center mall, which is four blocks long and 20 feet or maybe even 40 feet wide, and turn that into a community garden?" Our mission is to promote the sustainable development of Red Hook, not to develop the farm. The farm is the catalytic, inspirational, physical location for broader neighborhood change.

→ SEE LACERTE PAGE 216

→ SEE MARSHALL AND HODA
  PAGE 164

Is there a thinker, practitioner, movement, or body or work that personally inspires you or drives you?

Personally, I take my inspiration from a couple places. One is the kids in the community I live in. Currently, I have little kids knocking on my door at night asking if I can get them lemon sorrel. Most people don't know what lemon sorrel is, let alone Dominicans in a poor neighborhood in a public housing project. That, to me, is totally inspiring.

I draw inspiration from the space and the excitement that it gives other people. When people get onto this space, you can see them go "ah!" and they start making their own connections. Everybody's always got another idea for the space, which is awesome. We can't always respond to that, but to me that says that the potential is here on the planet and it is within people and they want to do it. That's great.

I draw a lot of inspiration from my staff and my colleagues, they teach me a lot.

Institutionally, Heifer International as an organization has a model that is respectful of people and the environment. At its best, it is very progressive and they tend to take account of issues of gender, equity, and environmental justice. In language and in impact—I know people who have been profoundly touched by Heifer International.

As a thinker, **Vandana Shiva**'s writing and personhood is inspirational. For me, the reason I say that is she writes in a way that my teens can read—and we're talking about kids that are 3 and 4 years under their reading level. As a thinker, as an activist, and as a person, I think she's an eloquent and lovely human being.

As a movement, I was really skeptical of Slow Food, to be honest, having come from the U.S. and experiencing it as a really elite institution. But I went to Tierra Madre—their biannual international gathering with 5,000 farmers from all over the world, with the vast majority of them from developing nations. I was touched, profoundly impacted by the insistence on human dignity and the dignity of the planet, and developing social and economic structures that preserve that.

→ SEE INTRODUCTION PAGE 11

Adapting the Botanical Garden into a Sustainable, Multicultural Resource

Interview with Susan Lacerte
Queens Botanical Garden, Flushing, NY

Anne Wiesen: How did Queens Botanical Garden become the garden that celebrates water?

We identified water as the unifying element at Queens Botanical Garden (QBG) because of its importance here on this site and because it is essential for all people in all parts of the world for our daily lives. We are located in one of the most ethnically diverse counties in the country, with over 130 languages spoken. In fact, 75 percent of Garden visitors speak a language other than English at home. Water functions as a metaphor for our common humanity.

With respect to the site, Mill Creek, a tributary of the Flushing River runs though this landscape and we thought at first that we would uncover it. But it's 13 feet underground, and it didn't make any sense. The water feature where you come in the main gate is an artistic and architectural reference to the tributary, and it functions as part of the water management system as well. There are a lot of flooding issues, and our goal is to manage 100 percent of water that falls from storms on site. The water in the channel will rise and fall with the weather conditions — if there is a drought the channel might be completely dry, but it would still be beautiful. So you may simultaneously relate to nature and enjoy a beautiful **architectural feature**.

I think the flooding issues are getting worse. Possibly global climate changes are causing these fast and furious storms that are flooding our arboretum. I've been here 13 years, and I've never seen flooding like

→ SEE MARSHALL AND HODA
PAGE 164

Watercourse traversing the site.
PHOTO USED WITH PERMISSION BY JEFF GOLDBERG/ESTO

we've had this last year. Our designers always have said that when there is less open space, flooding is worse and water runs faster off of hard surfaces likes streets and typical parking lots. The soil acts as a great big sponge. The idea is to slow down the water so that it doesn't overload the filtration systems. So in our parking garden that will be built next year, we're using permeable pavers so the water will percolate down into the soil and stay right here, on our site where it is needed and cherished. We want people to see these sustainable design innovations. So our [LEED platinum administration building and visitors' center] has a green roof that the public can get up to. And we'd like to start using rain barrels to catch water, something simpler that people can do at home.

Most large institutional gardens have not been in the forefront of sustainable design. How did Queens become engaged in sustainable building and operational systems design?

How QBG became engaged in sustainable design relates to how New York developed, and I see how we are a product of our times. The New York Botanical Garden (NYBG) was founded in the mid-1800s when we looked to England and more widely to Europe for knowledge of botany. And at the time of NYBG's founding, the emphasis in Europe was on plant exploration and research. So the need to have a space, a conservatory and a herbarium, to keep plants in order to study them was primary. So that's their legacy. Brooklyn Botanic Garden (BBG) was founded in 1911 and what they did was to take the model of rectilinear beds for plant families — the Legume family, the Compositae family, etc. — that were popular in European botanical gardens and they blended in horticulture. So BBG brought plant systematics together with aesthetics and combined both as a teaching tool.

Then you come to our garden, which was opened in 1948 and was developed from the Gardens on Parade exhibit of the 1939 World's Fair, which was all about innovation. It was here that Jackson & Perkins mail order roses were introduced is my understanding, and hydroponics. This "first" Queens Botanical Garden was in Flushing Meadows Corona Park. And then we were moved here in 1963 to make way for the World's Fair in 1964, during a time when ecology, conservation, and such ideas were becoming popular. So at this new place a bird garden, bee garden, woodland garden, and other ecologically based gardens were added.

**Sloped green roof allows
visitors easy access.**
PHOTO USED WITH PERMISSION
BY PHOTOGRAPHER JOHN SEITZ

In the 1990s Ashok Bhavnani, an architect, joined the board and he said to me: "Susan, you have an opportunity to be a leader among mid-sized botanic gardens in environmental design." And he articulated to some degree this sustainable, environmental idea, which wasn't common at the time. These ideas built upon what we already were. We picked [the architect and landscape architects] because of their interest in the environment and water and in trying to bring our cultural vision that we adopted in 1997, into the design. Our vision shows that we think of ourselves as "the place where people, plants, and cultures meet." When we started getting into design for this project, we expanded the idea of sustainability and we really tried to marry those two ideas — culture and sustainability.

Would you say your focus on supporting cultural diversity comes from your location here in Flushing?
Oh, absolutely, and in Queens at large. Our vision to celebrate diversity and the significance of the cultures in the communities around us evolved as we became integrated in the communities. We developed our board to be very diverse over time and we started working with whomever we knew locally. Queensborough Hall was very helpful in pointing us in the right direction — to the leaders in the Hispanic, Chinese, and the Korean communities. And with the help of these leaders we put several cultural advisory committees together.

We created a position called "Cultural Specialist," and offered an honorarium to three young people who had either been born in this country or had been born overseas but came here as a young child. They needed to understand both cultures. Each community wants to blend in and be part of America, but they also want to retain some of their own. We gave the cultural specialists an assignment to identify the 10 plants and the 10 holidays that are most important in the culture; the most important leaders in the community; and people from their community who are important in the press. And with their responses we published a book, "Harvesting Our History: A Botanical and Cultural Guide to Queens' Chinese, Korean and Latin American Communities" that captured some of these ideas. The Cultural Specialists were also responsible for successfully engaging leaders to invite guests to plant-related cultural events for each community.

What were some of those cultural events?

Working with the Hispanic community, we learned that color is very important so we set up a flower arranging event. The event was very formal with a professional florist addressing an auditorium of formally dressed participants. The florist created some very showy pieces, for example, he took white carnations, sprayed them blue and made a poodle out of them. Everyone in the audience loved it and clapped enthusiastically.

Then we had a Korean-born plant specialist from a botanical garden come in to give a talk in Korean and English about the plants that are important in the landscape from that part of the world. The Koreans have such a reverence for elders and for learning. Later, we helped the Korean community establish a Circle Garden of these important plants on the grounds here. The community raised $5,000 through an event called "Cosmos Night" over 3 consecutive years and that helped sponsor the Circle Garden. The cosmos is important in Korean celebrations.

In the Chinese community, years ago, we had Mark Lii, founder of Ten Ren Tea and Ginseng Company, hold a press conference at the Garden in Chinese in advance of our Four Seasons Chinese Tea Ceremony. The ambassador to Taiwan attended and said that Mark Lii is going to revolutionize tea drinking in America. Mark's got a teashop here in Flushing, in Chinatown, and in all the different Chinese sections of the city. I was introduced to Mark, he became a QBG Board Member, and that's how you build bridges.

We have relationships with certain cultural communities and we keep those and work with them. At this point we're doing a multilingual visitor brochure. I would like to see these cultural connections have a more physical presence in the garden.

We did some research where we took people to the market on Main Street because we had learned that people didn't always feel welcome walking into a store of another culture. Often times the shop owners don't speak English and because of this many of the signs are not in English either. But just by having tours with small groups of people that go into the market — to the Chinese Herb Shop, to the Indian Sari store, the Korean Specialty Shop — we made friends and the merchants loved it. And our members who might have been curious and passed by everyday, but never went in, made a connection. These are some of the

Having one's culture reflected publicly and powerfully can be a great stimulus to feelings of pride, acceptance, and positive integration.

ways we reach out to our communities, ways we value their culture and work, their ways of being a family and making home. In a sense, we bring the Garden to them!

In what ways does QBG support the health of the surrounding community?

Quite literally, we partner with the New York Hospital Medical Center, Queens, up the street. They also cater to largely Asian populations, and their approach to cross-cultural relations is very similar to ours. For instance, they respect language differences and so they'll send a Chinese-speaking doctor to come to the Garden and run health days where the doctor runs free cholesterol and blood pressure tests and talks to people about healthy lifestyles. We then sponsor Tai Chi here; every morning there are somewhere around 100 people practicing in the garden. It's so beautiful, and is a great traditional use of a garden. And you see diversity in the faces of the people who visit this garden every single day.

We've also done a project where we've put more Asian plants into the herb garden to educate people further about the Chinese herbs they may be taking. Having one's culture reflected publicly and powerfully can be a great stimulus to feelings of pride, acceptance, and positive integration. These are more about the social components that relate to health. Finally, the Medical Center has adopted a tree on their grounds. So there's cross-fertilization happening where the Center is using our method by planting and respecting trees, and we're hosting healthy days. We have a very good relationship.

How does your plant selection relate to your dual goals of sustainability and cultural diversity?

Native plants were selected for most areas because they are better adapted to the local conditions and so they need less care. Although they are beautiful, not everybody wants native plants. The brides and grooms who hold their ceremonies at the Garden want color. And concert planners want an outdoor venue. While the QBG arboretum, which is now managed as a meadow, has been the site of 5,000 person gatherings in the past, we can no longer do this because the plants in the meadow don't leave a place where that many people can gather.

Visitors practicing tai chi.
PHOTO USED WITH PERMISSION
BY PHOTOGRAPHER JASON GREEN

And there are some people who say we have gone backwards because they see a lot of 'weeds' out there. There's some education that needs to happen on both sides. This year I said I want an edge on that meadow so that people have the idea that it is deliberate. And we need to make it more beautiful. I'm not making a judgment that native plants aren't beautiful. But the public taste is for more for showy, colorful plants.

An impression that I've developed over the years working with people of different cultures is that a lot of people who come here to Flushing come from countries that are agricultural. Farming is a hard life. And they left the farm. They left those 12-14 hour days of hard labor and they don't want that kind of life anymore. They want to see something in the landscape that reminds them not of work, but of the celebrations, or peaceful moments they've known and can be inspired to continue.

What elements do you think are important in a 21st century park, botanical garden, or open space?
Well I wrote an article for "Public Garden" a year ago. I had some Cornell students to my house for dinner, and asked them what their idea of a

Watercourse (*above*)
continues through the
built landscape (*next page*)
and resolves in a
remediating bioswale.
PHOTOS USED WITH PERMISSION
BY PHOTOGRAPHER JOHN SEITZ

garden was. And what I came away with was that American gardens started off in this venerable European model where people would go to a garden to enjoy beauty and maybe to study plants. But technology has changed everything. People now expect information at their fingertips because they can go online, research, and learn so many things instantly. People are using gardens in so many different ways. I've read articles about putting a chip in a tree, and then with a handheld device, in whatever language they want, people can find out about that tree. I think that for gardens to be players in the world we've got to figure out: how can we continue to be relevant to people in this time of great technology? Does it make sense to emphasize gardens as a completely different experience from what's available to us electronically? Gardens are very local, as you know. And gardens move at a different tempo. Plants take time to grow. It could be the Garden's salvation because, I would think, the pendulum swings.

Would the components that make Queens Botanical Garden successful scale up to open space across the city?
Yes, what we are doing here would definitely scale up for larger areas of the city. Just think if more places had green roofs what a different city this would be! Just think if we did not treat all water to potable or drinkable standards but treated just what we needed and used water more efficiently. Just think if every building captured the sun's light and made it into energy for the building, just like plants turn the sun's light into energy for the plant. We'd have a cooler, more beautiful city, less flooding, fuller reservoirs and lakes, and less land used for all sorts of support facilities leaving more for open space, something I've found so important for my sense of spirit and beauty. We'd have a greener city and a healthier city. Not that I think what we have now is bad, it's just that it could be better, and doing so is within our grasp. It takes consciousness, determination and persistence, and all of us working together. We can lead in so many ways and I'm so proud that the Queens Botanical Garden is on the leading edge of this green phenomenon that is sweeping the nation. I hope everyone will join in!

Dialogue With Colleague:

How wonderful that QBG is connecting the personal experience of
health and well-being with the wider health of our city and planet.
These connections allow us to see ourselves as living creatures that
are members of an interconnected web of life. Demonstrating the
practical steps that help us locate our dwelling and work places
within a living ecosystem is a powerful tool for restoring our sense of
connection, responsibility, and spiritual heritage. Karl Linn once said
"From time immemorial, people of indigenous or land-based cultures
have celebrated their connectedness with nature as an integral part
of their daily lives. Free and enduring access to air, water, and land
assured their sustenance and survival." Linn felt places such as
community gardens and urban green spaces were the last remnants
of this experience in modern life. I think the botanical gardens serve
this function for many people in our city.

We are overstimulated and oversuggested as to what is beautiful.
It's hard to experience the subtle, awesome beauty of natural
landscapes. On one hand we want people to feel connected to a
garden experience, to be pleased by scent, color, shape. On the other
hand, so many people need the soothing experience of a meadow
or leaf strewn forest floor. I find urban residents are craving, are
starving for peaceful experiences in nature. Botanical garden visitors
often seek respite, quiet, and gravitate to the less designed areas,
or perhaps areas intentionally "less designed". How significant is the
preservation of a natural environment — one that looks and feels and
enacts the rhythms of our seasons — to a sustainable society? What
is the role of a botanical garden in providing this experience, through
design, landscape, and/or educational experience?

Susan Fields
GreenBridge Manager, Brooklyn Botanic Garden

The Re-Greening of Public Housing

Interview with Rob Bennaton
New York City Housing Authority Garden and Greening Program
New York, NY

Lindsay Campbell: How did the New York City Housing Authority Garden and Greening Program come about?

The New York City Housing Authority (NYCHA) was established in 1934 to provide affordable housing for low- and moderate-income families. The Garden and Greening Program was conceptualized as the Tenant Garden Program by Ira D. Robbins, a 1960s NYCHA board member, as a means to beautify housing grounds in an aesthetically pleasing and economically efficient way. Robbins learned from his visit to the Chicago Housing Authority that garden competitions were used to inspire beautification, except that the garden cultivators there were the grounds staff. He applied this basic concept in New York, emphasizing resident stewardship over staff maintenance. This vision of resident engagement as garden stewards has developed over the decades into more complex sets of issues and relationships linking to ownership, access, and control of one's immediate environment. Today, there are about 650 active gardens on NYCHA grounds and 3,000 gardeners, approximately 2,700 of whom are youth.

NYCHA Garden and Greening outreach coordinator Howard Hemmings (*left*) with Mr. Miller, a gardener at Mariner's Harbor houses in Staten Island.
PHOTO USED WITH PERMISSION BY PHOTOGRAPHER LLOYD CARTER, NYCHA

What kind of support does the program provide gardeners?

The five things that the Garden and Greening Program provides are:

- Free seeds in the spring and summer
- Free bulbs in the fall
- Technical assistance from Garden & Greening Program staff
- Reimbursement from the property management office in each development for up to $40/registered garden
- Some level of support from property management, which varies by development and can include: helping turn the soil, supporting the gardeners with watering hoses, lending of a shovel or two, etc. In addition to that, when management is willing and able to go retrieve it, they can get free leaf compost for those gardens to improve the soil quality from the Department of Sanitation.

There are a lot of different garden programs in the city, but NYCHA's centers around a garden competition whereas others do not. Can you talk a little bit about the strengths and weaknesses of having the competition as a key feature?

→ SEE STONE PAGE 122

Our program is very different from the New York City Department of Parks and Recreation **GreenThumb Program** and many other community gardening programs. Although NYCHA is moving toward a community gardening-like program, it's always been management's policy that these gardens do not belong permanently to a particular resident gardener or group of residents. The lands being cultivated revert back to the responsibility of a development's grounds staff when residents can no longer care for it because the condition of the grounds is ultimately the housing development management staff's responsibility. This presents some challenges for cultivating true long-term stewardship and a sense of ownership of the grounds.

Of the 650 gardens on NYCHA lands, approximately 500 gardens are officially registered with the garden competition and the remainder, often, are not registered but continue to be cultivated. Through NYCHA's citywide garden competition, the gardens are assessed for their horticultural cultivation practices, aesthetic value and/or alignment with a theme if a 'theme' garden. Judges look for signs of active garden maintenance, such as weeding, deadheading, mulching, amending soil, or using beneficial insects, and so, horticultural skills are encouraged

NYCHA Properties

Citywide map of the 343
NYCHA development sites.
There are approximately
2,600 acres of open space
on NYCHA grounds.
DATA SOURCE: NYC DEPT
OF PLANNING; MAP CREATED
BY JARLATH O'NEIL-DUNNE,
UNIVERSITY OF VERMONT

and rewarded. The competition as a starting point for a gardening program is something of a double-edged sword, both a strength and a weakness. It does promote healthy competition between residents, housing developments, and boroughs. But it also breeds the inevitable disappointment for those who don't win, and sometimes causes them to drop out of future competitions.

And has the program changed over time?

In 2002, after 40-plus years of running the garden competition, the rules were revised to reflect a changing understanding of the social function and value of these sites, as well as to improve them in terms of environmental sustainability. Howard Hemmings and I, both Community Coordinators, have sought to make it possible for gardeners to build and nurture social connections and environmental values through the gardens, not just within the housing developments, but by helping to support gardens as connectors with neighborhood residents as well. For example, an obsolete rule stipulated that perennials were not allowed in the gardens for reasons that are not clear. Well, perennials are now permitted in housing gardens because they are not only the sustainable foundations of a flower garden, but a resident's sense of connection to place that perennials can inspire is now understood as a positive. Perennials are also sustainable in the biological sense of returning annually from their roots with even greater growth, and providing needed resources and cover for native pollinators and birds. In the long run, we're hoping to develop these gardens as open spaces that will continue to be cultivated by resident membership groups through the generations. Over time, a resident membership base may develop that will seek to preserve some land for open space stewardship.

Focusing in on the theme of Restorative Commons, what do you see as the relationship between your gardening program and human health?

Gardening is a multifaceted activity that has social, environmental, aesthetic, and health impacts. Here are just a few examples of some of the benefits of gardening and open space that I have observed through this program:

St. Nicholas Houses, Harlem

At the St. Nicholas Houses in Harlem, they are developing a project to provide opportunities for physical activity within the landscape. The project involves developing a 1-mile walking path throughout the grounds, surrounded by plants and trees selected for easy maintenance, year-round interest, and pollinator value in partnership with the District Public Health Office of Harlem, the Neighborhood Open Space Coalition, NYCHA's Garden & Greening Program and the Department of Parks and Recreation. The Department of Health and "Take A Walk, New York!" program organize walking groups out of the senior centers to help address the dual concerns of diabetes and obesity. The New York City Department of Parks and Recreation aided the project by fully planting the perimeter trees on the street surrounding the development.

St. Nicholas Houses' current Manager Doreen Mack has many years of experience in the field, having worked with the citywide capacity-building nonprofit, Citizens Committee for New York City, and is an entrepreneurial advocate for her 15.3-acre grounds. Mack has stated, "Personally, I love flowers, I think they're calming. Gardening puts away some

of the drug activities because people congregate." Mack believes that for the stewards themselves, gardening provides exercise, activity, and a source of relaxation and pride. For those who simply see the gardens or walk by them, they provide visual interest, and reduce the amount of garbage dumped: even less mobile residents can benefit from looking out their windows at gardens. At St. Nicholas Houses, Mack hopes that eventually all 14 buildings plus the management office will have a garden; currently there are six gardens on the grounds. She believes that the 1-mile walking path can be a connector for those gardens.

Seniors using the "walking trail" at St. Nicholas Houses in Manhattan.
PHOTO USED WITH PERMISSION BY DAVE LUTZ, NOSC

- Horticulture can be used to help with anything from drug rehabilitation to relief from stress. In a city with 8 to 10 million residents, where people are always rushing, crowded on the subway, and generally stressed out, gardening can be an outlet to deal with that stress.

- Gardening is a form of recreation that is not too physically demanding and provides slow and steady exercise. John Reddick is a program consultant with the Trust for Public Land, a many-time judge of the Garden and Greening Program, and a consultant in the NYCHA community centers. Reddick noted, "Gardening is the only exercise some of these seniors get. It gets their day started in the early morning."

- Many of the active senior citizen stewards claim that they garden because it makes them feel good psychologically. Stewards are also motivated to garden because of the impact it makes on their communities. To quote Dr. Roy McGowan, former consultant of NYCHA, "Gardening is a nonconfrontational way to reclaim the land for productive and positive use."

Gardens can thrive even in the "found space" alongside parking lots and sidewalks; Saratoga Square in Brooklyn.
PHOTO USED WITH PERMISSION BY PHOTOGRAPHER LLOYD CARTER, NYCHA

- Vegetable gardens cultivate fresh, local food that offers an alternative to fast food and bodega snacks. They also serve an educational function in teaching children where vegetables come from — the soil in the ground rather than the supermarket. One of the challenges that our program faces is that some of the community centers grow food but do not harvest it. There is still a lot of technical assistance that needs to be provided to develop the gardens as viable urban agriculture sites.

- Plant cultivation offers an opportunity to connect with cultural roots. Many of the older gardeners grew up in the south, the Caribbean, or in other agrarian cultures, and value that way of life. Often, they want to plant collard greens and okra, or habanero chile peppers to have a taste of their cultural heritage, and recall their own roots. However, in the last 30 years there has been little turnover in residents and many of the people now living in NYCHA housing have grown up there. This connection with agriculture may be on the wane. Thus, we need to continue to develop interest in agriculture and land stewardship in light of the new populations we are serving.

Looking to the specifics of the Garden & Greening Program, how do the NYCHA gardens promote environmental sustainability?
One of the other main objectives of the garden program is to improve environmental quality as a whole, including: air quality, soil quality, and water quality. First, we now allow residents to plant perennials, including woody materials like trees and shrubs in addition to gardens, so that we're not only beautifying the open spaces and greening them up, but we're also fixing carbon.

Similarly, soil quality can be significantly improved with compost. We have reinstated what was in the original garden competition rules: soils, particularly those in first-year vegetable gardens, should be tested. With water quality, we're improving water bodies and waterways by retaining water so that it doesn't get onto the ground and become storm water runoff that carries nitrates and phosphates. Rainwater harvesting, a best management practice recently approved on a small scale by NYCHA's administration, is one step to doing that. Many of these issues are discussed in the book "Gardening for the Future of the Earth" by

Gardening is a form of recreation that is not too physically demanding and provides slow and steady exercise.

Shapiro and Harrison (2000), which describes how gardening can truly help to restore the healthy functioning of the earth.

What are some of the biggest challenges your program is facing now?

Historically, our programs were based out of the operations budget, which ultimately comes from rent and subsidies from the U.S. Department of Housing and Urban Development (HUD). Under the current Federal administration, funding for those subsidies has significantly decreased and NYCHA faces a very significant deficit. This and other factors have resulted in a vast reduction of the number of grounds maintenance staff in recent years.

Agency budget and staff reductions within the developments diminish capacity to assist gardeners with support such as turning soil and providing access to water sources. Grounds supervisors and staff must focus a great deal of attention simply on removing trash and debris with less person power then ever before. Ideally, the Garden and Greening Program could be expanded to include an outreach coordinator, as well as additional program coordinators serving each of the five boroughs of New York City. In the face of these significant funding cuts, NYCHA has rightfully focused its core resources on housing building upkeep rather than grounds maintenance and stewardship. Understandably so, as those upkeep needs are substantial.

It is critical that the above-named fiscal crisis not become an obstacle to resident garden stewardship because their voluntary garden maintenance can help NYCHA focus even more on its core mission of providing affordable housing services. By reducing the land maintenance burden on the shoulders of grounds staff, gardens in public housing can add value to existing open spaces, protecting public housing for both the affordable housing and ecological services it provides.

So, what next?

To better cultivate long-term stewardship of the NYCHA sites, the program is trying to build relationships between resident garden groups and local community resources. This presents one mechanism for overcoming physical and social barriers between public housing

Previous Page:
Rodriguez and McKay's flower garden at Patterson Houses in the Bronx.
PHOTO USED WITH PERMISSION BY PHOTOGRAPHER LLOYD CARTER, NYCHA

From MillionTreesNYC press release, April 2008:

Mayor Michael R. Bloomberg and David Rockefeller announced their joint pledge of $10 million to the MillionTreesNYC initiative to plant trees in public spaces including NYCHA developments and at City schools. This donation of private funds made to the Mayor's Fund to Advance New York City by Mr. Rockefeller and Bloomberg Philanthropies will allow over 18,000 trees to be planted throughout the five boroughs. Thanks to this donation, all nine of NYCHA's housing developments in East Harlem will be fully planted ahead of schedule and by the close of this year's tree planting season....As a result of this generous donation, more than 10,700 trees are slated to be planted on NYCHA property....Plantings will focus initially on sites in specially designated "Trees for Public Health" neighborhoods that have fewer than average street trees and higher than average rates of asthma among young people. These neighborhoods include Hunts Point, Morrisania, East New York, East Harlem, Stapleton, and the Rockaways. Funding will also be allocated for education and outreach efforts in these neighborhoods. In addition this gift will be used to help fund a new job training effort, the MillionTreesNYC Apprenticeship program, which will connect City youth to the numerous "green collar" jobs that PlaNYC is creating. Jobs related to tree planting and care are currently in high demand as a result of MillionTreesNYC, and the Apprenticeship Program aims to provide the skills that youth need to capitalize on well-paying career opportunities....The program will include NYCHA residents within the target population for training in jobs that involve the planting, pruning and stewardship of the trees.

Vegetable gardens and tree canopy at the Pink Houses in Brooklyn.
PHOTO USED WITH PERMISSION BY
PHOTOGRAPHER LLOYD CARTER, NYCHA

residents and their surrounding neighborhoods. Tenant associations are also an under-utilized, yet potential ally. These organizations serve as advocates for tenant rights on a wide range of issues, but relatively few of them are actively involved in the program. Corporate partnerships present new areas of opportunity as well. For example, Home Depot has supported resident gardening efforts with in-kind materials at the Polo Ground Houses Senior Center.

More good things are in the works, but all of them involve a need for the agency to broaden the programmatic scope of the Garden & Greening Program, as well as infrastructural support in terms of increased numbers of staff, vehicle access, and materials storage. Recent developments, including PlaNYC 2030, as well as the support of a strong environmental quality proponent in NYCHA's newly appointed agency Environmental Coordinator are positive signs of what is to come.

There is enormous opportunity to re-envision NYCHA landscapes as **dynamic, productive, ecosystems** serving the health and well- → SEE SEITZ PAGE 96 being of residents and the wider city. NYCHA oversees approximately 2,600 acres of open space with an estimated 46,000 trees and provides housing for a half-million tenants in 343 complexes across the five boroughs. NYCHA's existing social services infrastructure organizes residents and the surrounding neighborhoods around their 40 senior centers and 110 community centers that provide after school, summer day camp, and mature adult programs. Beyond these, NYCHA leases community facility spaces to a large variety of nonprofit agencies that operate in New York City public housing developments, including the noted "I Have a Dream" Program, the Institute for the Puerto Rican and Hispanic Elderly, and STRIVE, to name a few. There is great potential for improvement of environmental quality through the vast social capital that the New York City Housing Authority resident populations represent and the community facilities through which they serve.

Literature Cited

Shapiro, Howard; Harrison, John. 2000. Gardening for the future of the Earth. New York: Bantam Books.

Amending the soil to create a new garden bed at Astoria Senior Center, Astoria Houses in Queens. PHOTO USED WITH PERMISSION BY PHOTOGRAPHER LLOYD CARTER, NYCHA

The gardening program
is designed to serve entire
families.
PHOTO USED WITH PERMISSION
BY DAVORIN BRDANOVIC, AFSC

Gardens for Peace and Reconciliation

Interview with Davorin Brdanovic
American Friends Service Committee
Bosnia and Herzegovina

The Program

Lindsay Campbell: What are the goals of the American Friends Service Committee (AFSC) gardening program in Bosnia and Herzegovina?

AFSC has been registered in Bosnia and Herzegovina since 2000 and has focused on implementing an organic community gardening project. The basic goals of this project are to:

1. Support trust-building and reconciliation between different ethnic groups that were in conflict during the war in Bosnia and Herzegovina from 1992-1995 through multiethnic gardens.

2. Provide year-round material support for low income families through vegetable production.

3. Provide work/horticulture therapy for people with post-traumatic stress disorder (PTSD), disabled people, and people with mental health conditions.

4. Educate participants in conventional and organic agricultural production and environmental protection.

   Since the 2005 season, the project added an additional goal:

5. Support the development of independent community gardens through a national community gardening association.

When the project started, the idea was — if you want to do some reconciliation, you can't approach the person and say, "I have a wonderful project. Do you want to be reconciled?" It's true. First of all, to engage people in the gardens we address their most significant needs. It can be money, which is very often the case in Sarajevo. Aid organizations come often to hold roundtable discussions and they pay local people for their involvement. Here, there is a basic, urgent need for food security. Local people are coming to the gardens because it offers them a way to survive. Their benefit is the food harvest. What *WE* are harvesting is reconciliation. Of course, we don't tell them, "You are here for reconciliation."

Secondly, work therapy is *extremely* important. We have desperate people, destitute from the war — unemployed, at home, listening to politics, watching television — who need work therapy to feel they can work productively again.

Thirdly, we educate. We teach the gardeners agronomy. Most of these people have never raised crops or gardened before. They gain knowledge, they feel they can do something tangible and useful, they can produce something. Plus, they build friendships. Again, through *our harvest*, they develop friendships, they learn, and they will feel useful and part of a larger family.

LC: I understand that you don't say "get reconciled", but do you have programming or facilitation? Or is what's most effective really as simple as people working side by side?

This is why this program is unique. Everyone asks me, "Do you have a social worker? Do you have a therapist?" Really, you don't need it. They are sick of people who are paid to sit in front of them and tell them something that may or may not help them. There are simply so many nongovernmental organizations (NGOs), so many different international organizations with their own agenda in the rebuilding process.

You can solve the problem if you look and use your brain. Just watch what the people need. The perfect reconciliation for them is coffee time. We never have an official meeting. Me and my staff have a time and sit with them while they have a coffee. We speak with them. They always ask something, "Davorin, my house where I live is completely destroyed, do you know anyone who can make a donation?" So, I go to the Internet and look for an organization, check it for him and see if he is eligible for assistance.

Already the best thing is happening. We have two soldiers from opposite sides sitting in the garden and playing chess together. That's the best reconciliation, because, very soon, after a couple of chess

Local people are coming to the gardens because it offers them a way to survive. Their benefit is the food harvest. What WE are harvesting is reconciliation.

From AFSC website, www.afsc.org:

Established in 1917 in response to the human crisis of World War I, the American Friends Service Committee (AFSC) uses the Quaker values of nonviolence and justice to rebuild human lives and relationships. AFSC won the Nobel Peace Prize for 1947 on behalf of all Quakers worldwide in honor of their 300 years of work toward peace. Now headquartered in Philadelphia, AFSC has more than 40 office programs in the United States and in other parts of the world. This AFSC community "works to transform conditions and relationships both in the world and in ourselves, which threaten to overwhelm what is precious in human beings. We nurture the faith that conflicts can be resolved nonviolently, that enmity can be transformed into friendship, strife into cooperation, poverty into well-being, and injustice into dignity and participation. We believe that ultimately goodness can prevail over evil, and oppression in all its many forms can give way."

Tuzla Lotosice garden
is located in the center
of the town.
PHOTO USED WITH PERMISSION
BY DAVORIN BRDANOVIC, AFSC

parties and drinking coffee, they realize that even though they are on opposite sides politically, they are in the same position as people. They were both just told lies, lies, lies, and that's why they picked up the guns and started to fight. Now they are sitting together.

We never come and officially say, "Today we will have a meeting about reconciliation at 10:00 or 11:00." We only have meetings when there is something to discuss about agriculture, we post a notice saying, "today will be about composting or rainwater harvesting." Then they will know that everyone should come and participate. But, never meetings solely for reconciliation.

LC: In some ways it sounds like it's not just the work that you're doing, but it's also the common space that is important in this process.

It's a safe area. Because, inside, gardeners feel without weight.

They leave everything behind them when they come in the garden. The garden becomes an area that gives them absolutely a peaceful time. There's no stress inside. No one is forcing them to do anything. They're absolutely free to do whatever they want. They even bring their whole families sometimes. That's why we built the children's playground.

Erika Svendsen: What exactly are the therapeutic gardens?
They [AFSC and the German government] decided that the project is going to create new, well equipped demonstration gardens like the horticulture education gardens, but with each focusing on different mental and physical health issues in large part resulting from the war. We already have three therapeutic gardens inside our projects. There is 57 percent unemployment. And who's unemployed? The disabled. Let's be real. So there's a real need for gardens that can accommodate the disabled.

We plan to develop the therapeutic gardens and community gardens hand-in-hand, with a strong emphasis on establishing new gardens. This is the idea: We will partner with the health and disability organizations who already have land. I'll help them to organize a **therapeutic garden** → SEE KAMP PAGE 110 and will teach them how to become horticultural therapists. I'll also bring people without disability to the gardens at the disability organizations. We'll use the additional space that was not slated specifically for therapeutic uses to create a garden for the broader community. I'll demonstrate to the AFSC that I'm promoting reconciliation between mentally disabled people and healthy people! Now I have the perfect plan for how to get long-term community gardens to make reconciliation between members and disabled people.

Where did this idea come from? The Kula [prison] yard. We have a garden that is now temporarily closed. We were working with a **maximum security jail**. They gave us the land and I ran the program. → SEE JILER PAGE 178 I asked the director if he would open the gates and find prisoners who wanted to work in the garden. We started working with prisoners and after 1 year you could come in the garden and see a magnificent story. There were eight prisoners sitting in the garden and having coffee with the gardeners, because they have an interest, finally, to speak with someone. They bring them coffee, juice, cigarettes, but they help with weeding. It was Kula last year.

The Gardeners

LC: Does your program have a waiting list?

Yes, unfortunately, at this moment our waiting list is around 4,000 people.

LC: Do people consider working in the gardens a job? How do they think about it?

You need to know that all the gardeners are unemployed. And we also have a number of refugees, returnees, and retired people.

LC: Returnees are?

When you are a refugee you go somewhere and then when you come back you are a returnee. The reason that category is very important is that ethnic cleansing happened in Bosnia and Herzegovina. You know that. The leaders wanted to have "ethnically clean areas", with only one ethnicity in one area. Before the war, it was completely mixed. We are trying to help people come back because they still have property, land, apartments, flats, houses. Local politicians don't want them to return. When they return, it's impossible for them to find jobs and it's very difficult for them to get papers. That's our priority, to help them so that they at least have food before they begin working.

ES: What is the composition of the garden population? Do you have the same gardeners or do people change year to year?

All our gardens are multi-ethnic with the same percentage of the ethnicity as there was in the area before the war. That's what we are trying to do. By the way, just to explain, speaking of ethnicity, we have three major ethnicities: Serb, Croat, and Bosniak. By religion, Croats are 99.9 percent Catholic, Serbs are 99.9 percent Christian Orthodox, and Bosniaks are 99.9 percent Muslim. About 20 percent of our gardeners change each year. Normally, the refugees move away from the location of the garden and are therefore a difficult population to work with in the long term. We are trying to help refugees. All our gardens are multi-ethnic except for the garden in Srebrenica, because of the mass killing that happened there. The refugees of Srebrenica will never return because that place has such bad memories for them.

Parceling the Vogosca
garden into family units.
PHOTO USED WITH PERMISSION
BY DAVORIN BRDANOVIC, AFSC

"The perfect reconciliation
for them is coffee time."
Participants at the Stup
garden in Sarajevo.
PHOTO USED WITH PERMISSION
BY DAVORIN BRDANOVIC, AFSC

LC: So how do you identify good applicants?

We work with local organizations: Caritas, a Catholic organization; Merhamet, which is for Muslims; Dobrotvor for Orthodox; Red Cross; and the Center for Social Work. We tell them about our program and what we want to do. We ask them who wants to work and they help to find people who are actually able to work. Unfortunately there are people who are almost 90 years old who desperately want to apply, but are not fit for the work. You want to ideally find at least a larger family. After we receive the recommendations from the organization, we make a selection, and then sometimes we have a short interview — sometimes through the telephone. We check if all the data is correct that they give us. In the beginning, some people applied and looked fine on paper, but when you give them the seeds, they just took them and sold them on the market and never showed up again. Now we try to find families who really want to work and accept that the work is important. With our new therapeutic garden program, we will adjust the garden application form to ask: "Do you have the mind to work with the mentally disabled? Can you accept it?"

The Gardens

LC: Can you give more of a physical description of the gardens and farms? Talk about what they look like, what is grown there, that sort of thing.

First I'll tell you that we have 14 gardens this year; generally we have 20. We have two main gardens: one is in Stup and one in East Sarajevo, in Kula. We call these the main gardens because these gardens have all the equipment. In Stup, we have a greenhouse, a place where they can keep their tools, a place where they can dress and wash themselves. They have a kitchen where they can cook and prepare. They have tables for rest, they have a children's playground. A complete irrigation system was made. These two gardens are also gardens for education. We bring the gardeners from the other gardens for 1 or 2 days just to show them the things that they don't have in their gardens. It's around 10,000 square meters and has a 400-square-meter greenhouse. That garden is our first garden.

The difference from the other gardens is that all the others are "satellite" gardens. These gardens are just pieces of land and only one garden has a shelter. Mostly gardeners bring the tools with them, dig, do their work, and bring their tools back home with them. These gardens are not protected because the land is not given to us for the long term. It's not worth it to invest in something like making a fence or an irrigation system.

I need to describe the plots. We have 17 families inside and each member of the family has 50 square meters of land. After doing some research, we found that 50 square meters with 25 different types of vegetables, if it's well managed, fertilized, prepared, and taken care of, can give you exactly what one person needs for 1 year in terms of vegetables. They are small plots, and we're always mixing the plots so that people do not have the same plot of land every year. If member numbers of a family change — if a son marries and leaves there will be one less family member, so the plot size will change, and we move the borders using a small, thin rope.

LC: You can't be at all these gardens at once, do you have volunteers or staff who help you?
We have two women, two agronomists. I have an office manager and a maintenance worker at the two main gardens. That's all the employees we have: me plus four. And one more, an assistant to work on development. We tried with the volunteers, but the problem is this: when you have 57 percent unemployment, who will be a volunteer? People are starving! Now they will volunteer?

LC: Are any of the gardens permanently protected as parkland?
No. They have existed for longer than 5 years, and probably will exist another 3 years at least. But I don't have anything that is signed that says these gardens can remain for the long term, so it's risky to invest in such types of gardens.

All the gardens, which are working already, will be registered as independent NGOs. We will finish this year with nine registered gardens with garden leaders who have completed education on how to run a small NGO. We will partner them with brother and sister organizations. After this step, my idea is to create a community garden association of Bosnia and Herzegovina, an umbrella organization that serves all registered NGOs.

How did you get involved in this sort of work? And how has this work, in turn, affected you?

I don't have a background in agronomy. I studied economics, which actually helped me only for a few years before the war. During the war, there was no economy. I stayed in Sarajevo, which was under siege for 4 years. Under siege means: no food, no water, no electricity, no nothing. To survive there I had to do something to not be taken into the army. I knew how to use the computer and I had a small computer at home. The people who knew much more about computers left Sarajevo already....Bosnia was without a brain, without knowledge. Everybody left. I taught myself a bit about computers and started to repair them. I had to somehow find money because everything was gone. Money disappeared and wasn't worth anything, except for German marks. Fifty German marks, which is like $35-40 was 1L of oil or 1 kilo of sugar. One golden ring, was worth one box of cigarettes.

Then I started to work for different organizations, asking them to pay me. I know English, so I started working for different international organizations. Sitting at home, I began to think. "I have $1 in my pocket. How wonderful would it be to have another zero: $10 in my pocket?" I could have cigarettes or coffee. So I work, work, work, and I have that $10. "It would be absolutely wonderful to have one more zero: $100. I could have better food and even something to drink." Work, work, work, the zero comes. After 6 years finally I have enough money to buy a space and open offices, but I am working 24 hours a day with no time to meet, I don't have time for myself. I don't have anything." I called my wife and said, "Tomorrow we are going to sell the company. I want to do something that makes me happy. I'm unhappy for 6 years.

Then I started to work for AFSC, started this gardening project, and got my brain functioning again, full of ideas and new things. I know I'm doing something good that helps people and it makes me happy.

LC: And are the gardens in urban areas or in more rural, farm-like areas?

It depends. In Tuzla, we have a garden in the center of the town. In Doboj, we have a garden in the center of town. In Bosnia and Herzegovina, the towns are not so big. Sarajevo is around 600,000 people and the nearest town is around 10,000 people. So, its not big towns with suburban areas like in the US. Most gardens are in town, not in the center, but in town.

The Future

LC: What are some of the biggest challenges that you face?

The biggest challenge is to deal with the politicians and the post-war situation, which is still impossible. When they are on camera, politicians promise support to my program. But in reality, multi-ethnic gardens have the potential to negatively affect their political support base.

ES: We are all clear on how important your program is at this point in time after the war, but do you see it as something that will continue after the war for 20 or 30 years?

Generally, I'm an optimist. I think I can teach these garden leaders not to lose faith in finding the resources for this project, because it doesn't cost a lot of money to grow vegetables. Also, I think that gardens will increase in Bosnia and Herzegovina because there's so much land without ownership, or owners are missing or disappeared. Even in the town where our gardens are, near Stup and Kula, I see that people who didn't have the opportunity to be involved in the program are using the land near the airport to garden. I don't know if the idea came to them from these gardens or somewhere else. I have 2,000 people in the project who return back to their homes and talk about what they did in the garden with their friends and give a very positive picture. Consider that these 2,000 people have at least five friends or relatives who will then have a very positive opinion of the gardens — the idea is spreading. Maybe in invisible ways, I don't know. That's why, if you come to Sarajevo you can see areas that are starting to be gardens and I have no idea whose they are. They just come totally unorganized, have their plots, and garden on their own.

Dialogue With Colleague:

I have seen the same problem in countries all over the world and right here in New York City, people who don't have work they feel is important to ground and focus them, who feel depressed or disenfranchised, are easily manipulated by the media into blaming others for their problems. In Bosnia and with similar projects in Europe designed to provide work for refugee migrants we can see how community gardening can really provide an antidote to the feeling of powerlessness that makes people easy to manipulate. We like to think that situations like in Bosnia won't happen here in New York, but it hasn't been so many years since we have had riots based on race and social injustice. Perhaps our gardens, too, can provide an outlet for these feelings and a place for safe dialogue that will help prevent this type of problem from occurring in the future.

Both Davorin and I have been promoting the idea of a European Community Gardening Association, perhaps even a Worldwide Community Gardening Association. The more we travel for our jobs the more we meet people with similar problems of garden preservation, organizing and getting financial and governmental support. A global network is one way that we see community gardening projects being able to help each other to be more sustainable. In that light, some important questions I offer to Davorin are:

- Do gardeners have the skills and desire to manage their own projects?

- Will the association create a better political constituency for gardens?

- Will the association be sustainable in the long run without Davorin?

- What are the key benefits of the gardens being independent?

Edie Stone
NYC Parks GreenThumb

Working in the Kula prison
orchard.
PHOTO USED WITH PERMISSION
BY DAVORIN BRDANOVIC, AFSC

LC: Do you have someone or something who inspires you personally?

My grandfather was born in Sarajevo, my father was born in Sarajevo, and I was born in Sarajevo. And actually I'm living in the same apartment where I was born, still. This means that what inspires me in this work is recovering and rebuilding after the war. I live in a wonderful country, which is really the best country to live in — the former Yugoslavia.

I think that war is impossible. I don't care who is who. I don't ask, "Are my friends Muslim? Are they Orthodox? Are they Catholic? Are they Jewish?" I don't care. That was the last thing that would be mentioned. Who cares what religion or ethnicity you are? Somehow, after Yugoslavia broke up, it became the most important thing. "Who you are. Are you Muslim, Catholic, Serb, Croat, Bosnian, whatever?" When the war began, first in Croatia and then spread to Bosnia, I denied that it could possibly come to Sarajevo. When the first grenade fell in Sarajevo, I was leaning on the window. My wife said, "Do you see? When will you stop believing that the war is impossible?" I said, "Don't worry, the grenade is far away." I still wanted to believe that the life that I had, the friendships that I had, would continue. Now I think 80 percent of my friends live elsewhere.

Why did I stay? Why do I do this? For me, my mission is that someday I will see all my friends return. I KNOW that they will return one day, sooner or later. Somehow, it's destiny. I look at all these former Yugoslavian people all over the world: Canada, the States, Australia, Europe. They are creating a seed for a new generation of people. My generation will return and perhaps their children will stay. My mission is to provide a way to make this possible.

Appendices

About the Editors

This volume was researched, organized, and edited by Anne Wiesen, Executive Director of Meristem and Lindsay Campbell, Research Urban Planner at the U.S. Forest Service Northern Research Station.

Meristem, Inc., a 501(c)3 non-profit organization based in New York City, promotes nature's role in the improvement of human health and well-being by providing resources for understanding and developing Restorative Gardens and Commons.

Meristem hosts three program areas:

Restorative Gardens in healthcare settings are designed to link human wellness to the vitality of nature. Meristem's online library provides a literature review and case studies of gardens that exemplify restorative theory and design principles.

The Restorative Commons program launches the Restorative Garden model into public space—integrating design with a broad spectrum of emerging best practices in creating public places of health and renewal.

The Meristem Forum Series offers frameworks and venues for multi-disciplinary professionals and practitioners to exchange ideas and collaborate in shaping the Restorative Commons concept, practices and principles.

Meristem the botanical term, refers to specialized plant cells that both rebuild and initiate new structures at critical junctures of the organism. Meristem the organization, uses this model to catalyze nature's revitalizing potential in the landscape of public health.

Previous Page:
Green Apple Market,
Grand Army Plaza,
Brooklyn.
PHOTO USED WITH PERMISSION
BY PHOTOGRAPHER JOHN SEITZ

The U.S. Forest Service Northern Research Station's New York City Urban Field Station conducts research to answer the broad question, "How can urban greening be managed and understood as a tool for improving quality of life?" It does this in the country's largest metropolitan area, New York City. The Urban Field Station currently has three primary research areas:

> **Stewardship Mapping:** Fills the gap in understanding about how citizens serve as stewards by conserving, managing, monitoring, advocating for, and educating the public about their local environments (including water, land, air, waste, toxics, and energy issues); currently studying the organizational characteristics, social networks, and spatial distribution of thousands of civic environmental groups in New York City

> **Urban Tree Canopy:** Analyzing urban tree canopy and urban tree mortality issues to support the New York City's 30 percent canopy cover goal by 2030 and the efforts to plant 1 million new trees citywide on public and private lands

> **Environmental Literacy:** Research projects and partnerships aim to cultivate environmental awareness, knowledge, and skills of urban residents — with a particular emphasis on youth and students

The Urban Field Station partners with municipal managers to create innovative "research in action" programs to support urban ecosystem management. Forest Service scientists and partners conduct comparative research and disseminate knowledge throughout other metropolitan regions in the United States and globally. The Field Station links to a growing network of U.S. Forest Service scientists, facilities, and university cooperators focused on urban research.

Meristem Forum: Restorative Commons for Community Health

March 30, 2007
The New York Academy of Medicine

Agenda

8:00   **Arrival and Continental Breakfast**

8:30   **Welcome and Opening Remarks**

Anne Wiesen, Executive Director, Meristem

David Kamp, Principal, Dirtworks, PC Landscape Architecture

8:45   **Keynote Address: "Biophilia: A Neurologist's Perspective"**

Oliver Sacks, MD, New York University and Albert Einstein College of Medicine

9:15   **Landscape Architects, Physicians, and the Health of American Cities**

Robert Martensen, MD, Ph.D, Chair, Medical Humanities, Brody School of Medicine

9:50   **Nature and Psychological Well-Being**

Judith Heerwagen, Ph.D, Principal, Heerwagen and Associates, Seattle, WA

10:30   **Break**

10:45   **Discussion Session I**

Facilitator: Geri Weinstein-Breunig, Principal Cultural Waters, Madison, WI

11:45   **Lunch**

12:30   Creating Restorative Settings

David Kamp, Principal, Dirtworks, PC Landscape Architecture

12:45   Sustainability — Where the Rubber Meets the Road

Hillary Brown, Principal, New Civic Works

1:00   Urban Gardens: Details of the Restorative Infrastructure

John Seitz, Senior Associate, Cook + Fox Architects

1:15   Open Space & Well-Being: Cultivating Resilience

Erika Svendsen, Social Science Researcher, Urban Planner, USDA Forest Service

James Jiler, Director, GreenHouse on Riker's Island, New York Horticultural Society

1:40   Fresh Kills Landfill to Landscape:

Environmental and Human Health, A Reciprocal Relationship

Jeffery Sugarman, Associate Urban Designer, NYC Department of City Planning

2:00   Break

2:15   Discussion Session II

Facilitator: Geri Weinstein-Breunig, Principal Cultural Waters, Madison, WI

3:30   Summary of the Forum and Closing Comments

4:00   Adjourn

Meristem Forum: Restorative Commons for Community Health

March 30, 2007
The New York Academy of Medicine

Forum Participants
Affiliations current as of 2008

Noga Arikha, Ph.D
Scholar and Author, "Passions and Tempers:
A History of the Humors."

Rob Bennaton
Garden & Greening Program
New York City Housing Authority

Erika Blacksher, Ph.D.
RWJ Health & Society Scholar
Columbia University
Mailman School of Public Health

Hillary Brown, AIA
Principal, New Civic Works

Josephine Bush
Chair, Board of Directors
Urban Resources Initiative
New Haven, CT

Lindsay Campbell
Research Urban Planner
U.S. Forest Service
Northern Research Station

Candace Damon
Partner, Hamilton, Rabinovitch & Alschuler

Judith H. Heerwagen, Ph.D.
J.H. Heerwagen & Associates, Inc.
Seattle, WA

Jane Jackson
Director of Programming
New York Restoration Project

Kevin Jeffries
Deputy Commissioner for Public Programs
NYC Parks and Recreation

James Jiler
Director of the GreenHouse Program
The Horticultural Society of New York

David Kamp, ASLA, LF
President, Dirtworks, PC

Victoria Marshall, CLA
Principal, Till Design
Hoboken, NJ

Robert Martensen MD, Ph.D
Director, Medical History & Museum
National Institute of Health
Washington, D.C.

Charles McKinney
Chief of Design, Capital Projects
NYC Parks and Recreation

Nicole W. Moorehead
Chief of Staff to the Deputy Commissioner
for Public Programs
NYC Parks and Recreation

Elizabeth Barlow Rogers
President
Foundation for Landscape Studies

Oliver Sacks, MD
Albert Einstein College of Medicine
New York University Medical Center

Brian Sahd, Ph.D.
VP, Capital Construction and Real Estate
New York Restoration Project

John Seitz, AIA
Director of Sustainable Design
HOK

Robin Simmen
Manager, Brooklyn Greenbridge
Brooklyn Botanic Garden

Alex Stark
Architect and Feng Shui Master

Edie Stone
Director, GreenThumb
NYC City Parks and Recreation

Jeffery C. Sugarman
Associate Urban Designer
New York City Department of City Planning

Erika S. Svendsen
Research Social Scientist
NYC Urban Field Station
U.S. Forest Service

Annette Terry
Assistant Director
Department of Resident Support Services
New York City Housing Authority

Geri Weinstein-Breunig
Principal, Cultural Waters

Anne Wiesen
Executive Director, Meristem

Elizabeth Wiesen
Columbia University, Ph.D. Candidate
Dissertation: "Humoral Medicine and Ecology"

Contributor Biographies

Rob Bennaton

Community Coordinator, Garden & Greening Program, New York City Housing Authority, New York, NY

Rob Bennaton is a Community Coordinator with the New York City Housing Authority's (NYCHA) Garden & Greening Program within the Department of Community Operations. The objective of the Garden & Greening Program is to support public housing residents who beautify the grounds of housing developments in which they live by cultivating flower, vegetable or theme gardens. Bennaton is one of only two Community Coordinators working within the Housing Authority's Garden & Greening Program, which provides garden material resources and technical assistance to 600-plus New York City Housing Authority's residents' gardens. He has an extensive background in urban horticulture and habitat restoration and prior to NYCHA, has worked with the New York Botanical Gardens, the Natural Resources Group of the City of New York's Department of Parks & Recreation, Bronx River Restoration, and Bissel Gardens. Bennaton earned his undergraduate degree in biology and economics from Fordham University (2000), a commercial horticulture certificate in landscape management from the New York Botanical Gardens (2003) and a master's degree in urban planning with a focus on environmental planning from the Pratt Institute Center for Graduate Planning & the Environment (2007).

Davorin Brdanovic

Director, American Friends Service Committee Community Gardening Program, Sarajevo, Bosnia and Herzegovina.

Davorin Brdanovic is the Director of the American Friends Service Committee community gardening program in Bosnia and Herzegovina. The project focuses on reintegration of ethnic groups in Bosnia and Herzegovina by providing common space, productive work, and access to healthy food through gardening. Previously, Brdanovic studied economics and was self-employed in a computer repair business during and immediately following the Balkan War.

Hillary Brown, AIA

Principal, New Civic Works, New York, NY

Hillary Brown is principal of New Civic Works, which assists government agencies, institutional, and nonprofit clients, as well as private developers, in adopting sustainable design practices for their capital projects and programs. As former founder of NYC's Office of Sustainable Design, she oversaw its 1999 "High Performance Building Guidelines," and more recently envisioned and coauthored its "High Performance Infrastructure Guidelines." Brown has served on the national board and currently the New York chapter board of the U.S. Green Building Council. She teaches sustainable design at Princeton and Columbia University Schools of Architecture. Brown was a 2000 Loeb Fellow at Harvard University's Graduate School of Design, and a Bosch Public Policy Fellow in 2001 at the American Academy in Berlin.

Lindsay Campbell

Research Urban Planner, U.S. Forest Service
Northern Research Station, New York, NY

Lindsay Campbell is an urban planning researcher with the U.S. Forest Service, Northern Research Station assigned to the New York City Urban Field Station. She is co-researcher with Erika Svendsen on the Stewardship Mapping and Assessment Project (STEW-MAP), a study of 3,000 environmental groups in New York City. Svendsen and Campbell were awarded the 2008 EDRA/Places Award for Research for their work on the Living Memorials Project, a project to understand changes in the use of the landscape and natural resources in response to September 11, 2001. She began working for the Forest Service on a one year fellowship, funded by the Princeton Class of 1956. She has a bachelor's degree from Princeton University's Woodrow Wilson School of Public Policy and International Affairs. Campbell has a master's of city planning from the Massachusetts Institute of Technology, where she was a MIT-USGS Science Impact Collaborative Graduate Fellow.

Judith Heerwagen, Ph.D.

Principal, J.H. Heerwagen & Associates,
Seattle, WA

Judith Heerwagen is an environmental and evolutionary psychologist. Her research and writing have explored the relationship between nature and people from an evolutionary perspective. With ecologist Gordon Orians she has used habitat selection theory as a basis for understanding the strong emotional bonds that connect humans to natural places and elements, such as flowers, water, trees, and animals. Her work with Orians has appeared in "The Adapted Mind" (Oxford University Press 1992) and "The Biophilia Hypothesis" (Island Press 1993). Her recent work, with Bert Gregory, President of Mithun architects in Seattle, has begun to explore how features and attributes of nature can be used to design buildings and spaces that are healthy and appealing. She has lectured widely on sustainability and biocentric design and coedited a book "Biophilic Design: Theory, Research and Practice" (John Wiley 2007). In 2005 the American Society of Interior Designers selected her as an "environmental champion."

Dil Hoda

C.E.O, Tern Group, Hoboken, NJ

Dil Hoda is the founder and C.E.O. of Tern Group, a real estate development company focused on creating sustainable communities. Currently he is developing a 7-million-square-foot mixed-use project on a closed landfill in Elizabeth, NJ. His projects focus on blending financial, environmental, transportation, and arts-related elements into cohesive, sustain-able systems. He has also developed the Monroe Center for the Arts, a culturally anchored mixed-use development in Hoboken, NJ. Prior to his development activities, Hoda worked as a banker in New York and as a civil engineer in India and Saudi Arabia. Hoda teaches real estate development at New York University's Real Estate Institute. He has a master's of business administration degree from University of Pennsylvania's Wharton School.

James Jiler

Former Director, GreenHouse on Rikers Island,
New York, NY

James Jiler is former Director of The
Horticultural Society of New York's GreenHouse
Program, a jail-to-street horticulture program
at New York City's jail complex on Rikers Island.
GreenHouse provides men and women inmates
with vocational skills, science learning and
horticultural therapy through landscape design,
garden installation and greenhouse and garden
maintenance. Once released ex-offenders have
the opportunity to continue developing their
horticulture skills as paid interns with HSNY's
GreenTeam. Graduates of GreenTeam are
encouraged and helped to find full-time
employment with private businesses, nonprofit
organizations or city and state agencies as
professionals in the field. His work has been
featured in a recent documentary called the
"Healing Gardens" and has also been featured
in "The New York Times", "The Daily News",
"Newsday", "The Source", and "National
Audubon Magazine" among others. Jiler is
author of the book "Doing Time in the Garden"
(New Village Press 2006), which details the
GreenHouse approach to rehabilitation and
explores the role of gardening in jails and
prisons around the country. James Jiler is
currently residing in Miami, FL, helping to
establish similar environmental programs for
the Florida State Prison system through
Artspring — a nonprofit that provides an arts
curriculum to incarcerated women and youth.
Jiler holds a master's degree in forestry from
Yale University.

David Kamp, ASLA, LF

President, Dirtworks, PC Landscape Architecture;
Meristem Co-founder and Board Member,
New York, NY

In his 30 years of practice, David Kamp's
contributions to landscape architecture have
encompassed planning, large-and small-scale
design, research, writing, teaching, and public
service. Kamp has collaborated with many of
the country's leading architects on projects
throughout the United States and abroad,
including his leadership as Associate in Charge
of Australia's New Parliament House. Kamp
has engaged in continuing research from
self-directed studies in healthcare and the
human condition as a Loeb Fellow at Harvard
University. As the first landscape architect
invited as an artist-in-residence at the
MacDowell Colony, America's oldest and most
prestigious artist colony, Kamp developed
a series of prototypical gardens serving a
range of individuals with special needs. An
advocate and practitioner of ecologically
sound design, Kamp contributed to the
"Green Guide for Healthcare Construction."
Several American and international television
documentaries have featured Kamp and
the projects of Dirtworks. In 2006, he was
featured in "Recreating Eden," a Canadian
produced documentary series exploring the
role of gardens in the lives of people. Kamp
was featured in "GardenStory" on PBS in
spring 2008 showing how restorative gardens
support health and enrich the lives of patients,
visitors, and staff in healthcare facilities.

Susan Lacerte

Executive Director, Queens Botanical Garden
Susan Lacerte has served as Executive Director of the Queens Botanical Garden since 1994. She has a unique combination of extensive horticultural and financial experience. Lacerte was Director of Adult Education and Public Programs at the Brooklyn Botanic Garden from 1985–1990 and worked for the New York City Council Finance Division as a budget analyst from 1991–1994. Lacerte has written botany, horticulture and geographic entries for The Concise Columbia Encyclopedia, the Macmillan children's dictionaries, and The Cambridge Gazetteer of the United States and Canada. She holds a master's in Public Administration from NYU Wagner School of Public Service and a B.S. in Environmental Horticulture, University of Connecticut.

Victoria Marshall, CLA

Founder and Principal, TILL, Hoboken, NJ
Victoria Marshall is both a landscape architect and urban designer. She studied at the University of Pennsylvania PennDesign (1997) and has taught at that school as well as Parsons The New School for Design, Columbia GSAPP, Pratt Institute School of Architecture, The University of Toronto ALD, and Harvard GSD. Her current research aims to translate urban ecology frameworks as urban design models in the U.S. East Coast Megalopolis. This work is manifest in the recently published book in collaboration titled "Designing Patch Dynamics: Baltimore." Marshall is also the founder of TILL (2002) a mainland-based landscape architecture practice that offers professional design services for contemporary landscapes such as brownfields, waterfronts, rooftops, and landfills. TILL's design approach is based in disturbance ecology which is best described as a practice that engages different stakeholders' input and preferences over multiple time cycles and results in designs that are spatially heterogeneous, distributed, and responsive with socio-natural systems.

Robert Martensen, M.D., Ph.D.

Director, Office of NIH History and Museum, National Institute of Health, Washington, D.C.
With perspectives drawn from his training in medicine and history, Robert Martensen's recent work examines mind-body relationships in Western thought in different contexts. For general readers, he has just completed writing "The American Way of Illness: Eight Tales from the Front Lines" (Farrar, Straus & Giroux in press). His 2004 book, "The Brain Takes Shape: an Early History" (Oxford) explores cultural debates that took place during the Scientific Revolution concerning the physiological basis of reason, emotion, and personhood. In collaboration with artists including Robert Irwin and landscape architect David Kamp, Martensen also has explored Western perceptions of nature and the role of gardens in healing. His previous work has been supported by the National Institutes of Health, the Wellcome Trust, and a Guggenheim fellowship.

Ian Marvy

*Executive Director, Added Value and Herban
Solutions, Inc., Brooklyn, NY*

Ian Marvy is a co-founder and the current
Executive Director of Added Value and Herban
Solutions, Inc. Added Value's mission is to
promote the sustainable development of Red
Hook (Brooklyn) by nurturing a new generation
of youth leaders. Prior to founding Added
Value, Marvy spent 15 years organizing youths
to become a positive force for social change
in post-industrial cities and towns such as
Holyoke, MA, Camden, NJ, and Philadelphia,
PA. Marvy is a graduate of Hampshire College
where he majored in political theory and
American history, receiving the Peace and
World Security Scholars Fellowship and the
Social Justice Scholarship. Marvy arrived in
New York City in 1998 and worked for 2 years
designing service-learning programs for youth
caught in the juvenile justice system. In the
winter of 2000, he began working with three
teenagers and Michael Hurwitz (Added Value's
cofounder and now the Director of New York
City GreenMarkets) to create Added Value.
Marvy was a 2002 Echoing Green Fellow.
In 2004, Marvy and Hurwitz were honored
as Petra Foundation Social Justice Fellows.
In 2007, the duo were recognized as Union
Square Awardees and were recipients of
the 2007 Glenwood Harvest Awards in honor
of their efforts to grow a new generation
of leaders.

Colleen Murphy-Dunning

*Director, Urban Resources Initiative at the
Yale School of Forestry & Environmental Studies,
New Haven, CT*

Colleen Murphy-Dunning is the Director of
the Urban Resources Initiative (URI) at the
Yale School of Forestry & Environmental
Studies. Through the URI program, Yale
graduate students learn community
forestry methods while contributing to the
neighborhoods of New Haven. URI supports
members of the New Haven community to
become active stewards of their environment
through two interconnected programs:
Community Greenspace, a community-based
neighborhood greening program; and Open
Spaces as Learning Places, an urban-based
environmental science program. Murphy-
Dunning also partners with faculty to instruct
courses in environmental justice, monitoring
and evaluation methods, and urban ecology.
Prior to coming to Yale University in 1995, she
taught agroforestry extension courses at the
Kenya Forestry College. Murphy-Dunning holds
a master's degree in forestry from Humboldt
State University.

Oliver Sacks, M.D.

*Columbia University Medical Center, Professor
of Neurology and Psychiatry; Columbia University
Artist; Albert Einstein College of Medicine
and New York University School of Medicine,
Professor of Neurology, New York, NY*

Oliver Sacks is a physician and author known
for his elegantly written neurological case
studies. Both as a physician and as a writer,
Sacks is concerned with the ways in which

individuals survive and adapt to different neurological diseases and conditions, and what these experiences can tell us about the human brain and mind. His books include "The Man who Mistook his Wife for a Hat", "Awakenings" (which inspired the acclaimed 1990 film as well as a play by Harold Pinter), and more recently "Uncle Tungsten and Oaxaca Journal." Sacks is a professor of neurology at the Albert Einstein College of Medicine and at the NYU School of Medicine, and a member of the American Academy of Arts and Letters. His work has been supported by the Solomon R. Guggenheim and the Alfred P. Sloan Foundations. He is currently at work on a book about music and the brain. "The New York Times" has referred to Sacks as "the poet laureate of medicine," and in 2002 he was awarded the Lewis Thomas Prize by Rockefeller University, which recognizes the scientist as poet.

John Seitz, AIA

Director of Sustainable Design, HOK, New York, NY
At HOK Seitz is responsible for integrating sustainable design through the New York office's projects and operations and leads the office's sustainable masterplanning initiatives. His 20 years of experience in the design, project management and delivery of sustainably-designed high-performance buildings has included positions with Cook + Fox Architects, Croxton Collaborative Architects and William McDonough. He managed the compilation of the World Trade Center Sustainable Design Guidelines and the design of numerous award-winning sustainable buildings including the University of Florida, Rinker School of Building Construction and Chattanooga Development Resource Center. Seitz is a member of the AIA, the USGBC, is on the Meristem Board of Directors and has taught at New York University and Harvard University. Early in his career John spent 2 years in Papua New Guinea aiding villagers in the construction of rainwater catchment systems. An avid urban gardener, Seitz helped build community gardens throughout NYC after his architectural studies at MIT and Carnegie Mellon.

Edie Stone

Director, New York City Department of Parks and Recreation GreenThumb Program, New York, NY
Edie Stone has been the Director of the New York City Department of Parks and Recreation GreenThumb Program since 2001. GreenThumb supports community efforts to create and maintain over 500 community gardens throughout the city. Prior to joining GreenThumb, Stone worked for the Council on the Environment of New York City where she was active in helping community gardeners organize politically to work toward preservation of their garden sites. Stone is a former editor of the Council on Economic Priorities "Corporate Environmental Data Clearinghouse" and a contributor to the organization's publication "Shopping for a Better World." Stone is a graduate of Barnard College of Columbia University and the University of Michigan School of Natural Resources.

Jeffery C. Sugarman, RA

Associate Urban Designer, City of New York Dept. of City Planning, New York, NY

Jeffrey Sugarman is an Associate Urban Designer at the New York City Department of City Planning. Most recently he was Project Director for the Fresh Kills End Use Master Plan for the transformation of a 2200-acre closed landfill on Staten Island, NY into a new park and nature preserve. His work on numerous large-scale development plans and zoning initiatives has emphasized the integration of architecture and open space. These include Arverne, a mixed-use community plan for 7000 apartments with neighborhood and regional parks in Far Rockaway, Queens; the NYC Comprehensive Waterfront Plan; and Zoning and Urban Design Regulations for mandated publicly accessible, waterfront open space. He studied environmental design with Laurie Olin and Carol Franklin at the University of Pennsylvania before receiving his M.Arch. from the University of Virginia in 1980.

Erika Svendsen

Research Social Scientist, U.S. Forest Service, Northern Research Station, New York, NY

Erika Svendsen is a social science researcher with the U.S. Forest Service, Northern Research Station assigned to the New York City Urban Field Station. Svendsen is the former director of the NYC Parks Department's citywide community gardening program, GreenThumb. Prior to her work in New York City, she worked for The Rockefeller Foundation's Global Environment Program and LEAD International. She serves on the advisory boards of Meristem, Inc. and Groundwork USA. Svendsen is a graduate of Yale University School of Forestry and Environmental Studies and is currently a doctoral candidate at Columbia University's Graduate School of Architecture, Planning and Preservation.

Anne Wiesen

Executive Director, Meristem

Anne Wiesen co-founded Meristem in 2001 to create new possibilities for her interests in nature's role in human health and well-being. Through Meristem, she has been able create innovative partnerships with leading medical, design and land management practitioners to join community health concerns with the revitalization of local landscapes. The Restorative Commons initiative extended these considerations to the design and programming of urban public spaces. Wiesen's studies in medical ethnobotany (MS, New York University), human development (M.Ed., Harvard University) and landscape design (New York Botanical Garden), helped shape Meristem and continue to influence her cross-cultural medical theory research and its applications to plant medicine practices, restorative garden design, and urban planning.

Campbell, Lindsay; Wiesen, Anne. 2009. **Restorative commons: creating health and well-being through urban landscapes.** Gen. Tech. Rep. NRS-P-39. Newtown Square, PA: U.S. Department of Agriculture, Forest Service, Northern Research Station. 278 p.

A collection of 18 articles inspired by the Meristem 2007 Forum, "Restorative Commons for Community Health." The articles include interviews, case studies, thought pieces, and interdisciplinary theoretical works that explore the relationship between human health and the urban environment. This volume is a joint endeavor of Meristem and the U.S. Forest Service Northern Research Station as they work to strengthen networks of researchers and practitioners to develop new solutions to persistent and emergent challenges to human health, well-being, and potential within the urban environment.

KEYWORDS: civic stewardship; natural resource management; design with nature; neighborhood resilience; sustainable city; green infrastructure; ecology.

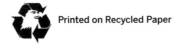 Printed on Recycled Paper